SIMPLE CUISINE

SIMPLE CUISINE

THE EASY, NEW APPROACH TO FOUR-STAR COOKING

■

JEAN-GEORGES VONGERICHTEN

PHOTOGRAPHS BY TOM ECKERLE

PRENTICE
HALL
PRESS

NEW YORK ■ LONDON ■ TORONTO ■ SYDNEY ■ TOKYO ■ SINGAPORE

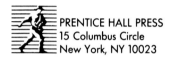 PRENTICE HALL PRESS
15 Columbus Circle
New York, NY 10023

Library of Congress Cataloging-in-Publication Data

Vongerichten, Jean-Georges.
    Simple Cuisine / Jean-Georges Vongerichten.
        p.   cm.
    ISBN 0-13-195059-2
    1. Cookery, French.   I. Title.
TX719.V66   1990
641.5944—dc20   89-78154
                                                      CIP

Designed by Patricia Fabricant

Manufactured in the United States of America

10 9 8 7 6 5 4 3 2 1

First Edition

Page i. Millefeuille of Roquefort and Boursin

Pages ii to iii. A section of vegetable juices and flavored oils—building blocks of my cuisine—and the essentials of good cooking, exquisitely fresh produce

Page iv. Roast beef with tomatoes, greens and Chive Oil on toasted bread; poached salmon with Basil Oil. Oils, in bottles, *from left to right:* Basil, Chive and Paprika Oil.

ACKNOWLEDGMENTS

■

I want to thank a few of the people who helped me bring forth my first book.

Many thanks to all the cooks in my kitchen who assisted me these past four years in developing the new styles and concepts I now bring you.

To Lois Freedman, one of my cooks, special thanks for helping me translate and unravel the mysteries of ingredients and preparation into the simplicity of these recipes.

To my friend Michael Futterman, many thanks for his advice, help and constant encouragement during the year-and-a-half adventure of writing *Simple Cuisine*.

CONTENTS

■ C O N T E N T S ■

INTRODUCTION
A NEW APPROACH TO FAST COOKING

■

Asked by many friends, magazines and newspapers for my recipes over the last few years, I realized finally that my new style of cooking is ideal for the home cook. It is the very answer for anyone who wants to prepare memorable meals but feels put off by complicated recipes. To these home cooks, I heartily dedicate this book.

By 1987, with Restaurant Lafayette open one year and a three-star award from the *New York Times*, I began experimenting with a new approach. I was looking for a way to give foods more intense flavor, as well as make them lighter, fresher. As it happened, the dishes I discovered along the way were also astonishingly rapid to prepare.

I dropped those elements of classic and nouvelle cooking that take considerable time and effort. My new cuisine relies on the simplicity of lightly steamed and sautéed foods, and limits the use of cream, butter and flour. With a handful of simple sauces and broths (today I think of them as my "basics"), I realized a virtually limitless variety of fabulous combinations and, in the process, shaped a new approach to cooking.

This new approach maximizes ease of preparation, lightness and visual appeal. Here is how it works: To replace traditional basics of French cooking (such as time-consuming stocks and butter-thick sauces), I use "building blocks." They are:

JUICES   VINAIGRETTES   FLAVORED OILS   BROTHS

A fifth basic ingredient, phyllo dough, replaces puff pastry. With these building blocks, everything from appetizers and seafood to poultry and meats can be prepared with a thrillingly fresh point of view and—here's the best part—in very little time. Innovative seasonal fruit desserts, ice creams, sorbets and granités were a natural extension of our new approach, and many are included in this book.

Our customers at the restaurant were very enthusiastic about the new and simple directions we were taking. It was always my hope to please not just those people who take food very seriously but the diner who samples our food on a birthday or other special occasion. We must have been doing something right, for in April of 1988, the *New York Times* awarded us its highest rating: four stars.

Before preparing the dishes I offer in this book, make a few of the basics first—a vegetable juice, a flavored oil, a vinaigrette, a vegetable broth. Once you have prepared a few of the building blocks, you will know essentially all there is to know about how these basics can become a mainstay of your everyday cooking. You can come home at the end of the day with a nice piece of fish or steak and, ten minutes later, sit down to a marvelous meal. Turn to page 93, "Simple Sautés and Steamed Dishes," and see how easy it is to quickly sauté or steam fish, shellfish, poultry or meat and combine it perfectly with the basics. With three or four flavored oils and vinaigrettes in the cupboard and refrigerator (and with the rapid preparation of juices and broths), you'll immediately feel freer to cook not only more creatively, but more quickly too.

In addition to chapters that highlight the building blocks, I've included a chapter on foie gras. It is probably the most luxurious food known to mankind—one I wouldn't want to live without—and simpler to prepare than you might think. Also included are chapters that reflect my love of Oriental flavors, some rather special side dishes, my interpretation of some American classics (such as hamburgers, shrimp cocktail and a tuna "sandwich"), and desserts, of course.

Finally, I've included lots of menus. Use them for inspiration or to help with those times we all have occasionally, when we just run out of ideas. If you need a menu for a special occasion, or want to put together a wonderful meal in thirty minutes or less, look here.

Most of my recipes are uncomplicated. Some take a little more time than others, but I think you'll find the results speak for themselves. A word on presentation: It is something that has always been important to me, and you should feel free to experiment, just as you would with seasoning, to suit your own taste and please yourself.

It hasn't been easy to set out on a new path in cooking, particularly when the cuisine of my mentors and fellow chefs is so special. I hope that the ideas and small innovations you find in these pages inspire you as they have me, and that they become a comfortable and exciting part of your life in the kitchen.

Most important to me is that you let your imagination go—and have fun.

Amitiés Gourmandes,

Jean-Georges Vongerichten
New York City

BUILDING BLOCK: JUICES

The primary element of my cuisine is the use of vegetable juices—and the occasional fruit juice—simple, richly flavored sauces by themselves and in combination with flavored oils. One morning, several years ago, I prepared myself a glass of carrot juice as a little "pick-me-up," and suddenly I realized that—with only a little seasoning—it would serve as a perfect complement to shellfish. I prepared it as a sauce and it was exquisite. This new preparation had the three characteristics a sauce needs to be great: body (texture), seasoning and acidity. This carrot sauce, my first vegetable juice recipe, appears on pages 2 and 11.

The vegetable juices must be made with a vegetable juicer. Juicers I have used and recommend are the ACME Model 6001, the Waring Model PJE 40 or the Champion. All are available in kitchen supply stores featuring food processors and similar equipment. Remember: Vegetable juices can't be made with citrus juicers or standard food processors, because they don't separate juice from pulp.

The preparation of the juice sauces takes less than 5 minutes. The vegetables and fruits used in the recipes that follow are:

CARROTS	ZUCCHINI	CELERY	LEEKS	PEPPERS (YELLOW, GREEN AND RED)	RADISHES
FENNEL	ASPARAGUS	BROCCOLI	BEETS	PINEAPPLES ORANGES	GRAPEFRUIT

Each recipe that calls for a vegetable juice will specify the amount of the vegetable needed to make the appropriate amount of juice. Preparation of a vegetable juice sauce begins by feeding the raw, scrubbed vegetable through the juicer as the manufacturer directs. Always use the recommended amount of juice. If more is needed, run another vegetable through the juicer. To the raw juice we add some seasoning and a touch of oil or a little butter. This mixture is cooked over low heat until it just boils. It's better to prepare the sauce just before it's needed.

Shrimp in Spicy Carrot Juice (page 11) garnished with a Carrot Basket (page 197), Sea Scallops with Zucchini Juice (page 9). Juices, in bottles, *from left to right:* carrot, beet, pineapple, asparagus, tomato, celery and pink radish juice.

NOTE: Most vegetables contain a considerable amount of water, and the sauce may separate. Don't worry. Leave the sauce on very low heat for a few moments while whisking briskly. Whisk again just before serving.

EXAMPLES:

SPICY CARROT JUICE

Peel 10 medium carrots.

Put the carrots through a juice extractor. You should have 2 cups of juice.

In a saucepan, combine the carrot juice and a pinch each of ground cinnamon, ground clove, ground nutmeg, salt and cayenne pepper. Add 4 tablespoons cold sweet butter, cut into pieces.

Bring the mixture to a boil over medium-low heat, whisking constantly.

As soon as the sauce reaches a boil, take it off the heat. If not serving it immediately, keep it warm over low heat.

MAKES 2 CUPS (USE ½ CUP PER SERVING)

ZUCCHINI JUICE WITH THYME

Put 4 large zucchini (unpeeled) through a juice extractor. You should have 2 cups of juice.

In a saucepan, combine the zucchini juice, ¾ cup extra virgin olive oil and 2 tablespoons whole fresh thyme leaves or 2 teaspoons dried.

Bring the mixture to a boil over medium-low heat, whisking constantly.

As soon as the sauce reaches a boil, take it off the heat. If not serving it immediately, keep it warm over low heat.

MAKES 2 ¾ CUPS (USE ½ CUP PER SERVING)

In addition to their use in the recipes that follow, the vegetable juice sauces complement perfectly the quick sautés and steamed dishes of chicken, veal, fish and shellfish on pages 93 to 105.

SMOKED SALMON CUSTARD WITH FENNEL JUICE

Use a steamer when preparing any custard. When you bake a custard, even using a water bath (a *bain marie*), you will have a grainy custard with little holes. Steaming, a method that uses indirect heat, avoids this and gives you perfectly smooth results. If nonstick ramekins are not available, use ceramic ones lined with plastic wrap.

> 1 cup diced smoked salmon (8 ounces)
> 1 cup milk
> 2 eggs
> 1 tablespoon plus ½ teaspoon fresh lime juice
> Salt and cayenne pepper to taste
> 5 medium bulbs fennel, coarsely chopped (leaves reserved for garnish)
> 2 tablespoons sweet butter plus additional butter for the molds
> ¼ teaspoon fennel seeds

Put the salmon and milk in a food processor or blender. Process to a smooth purée.

Whisk together the purée, eggs, 1 tablespoon lime juice, salt and cayenne pepper until well combined.

Put the fennel through a juice extractor. You should have 2 cups of juice. Add ½ teaspoon lime juice.

Smoked Salmon Custard with Fennel Juice, garnished with salmon roe

Lightly butter four 2-ounce nonstick ramekins and fill them with the salmon mixture. Place the ramekins in a steamer and cover tightly. Steam for 7 minutes or until the custard is set. Unmold onto serving plates, using a sharp knife if necessary to help loosen the sides.

Heat the fennel juice mixture, butter and fennel seeds just to boiling. Spoon a little of the sauce over the custard. Garnish with fennel leaves.

SERVES 4

YELLOW PIKE WITH CELERY JUICE

Yellow pike is the natural cross of northern pike (brochet) and perch. Brochet has too many bones to enjoy as fillets, but it is superb in quenelles or a fish terrine. Yellow pike is a wonderful fish with the flavor of northern pike and the finesse of perch.

1 bunch celery, chopped (do not peel)
6 tablespoons heavy cream
4 seven-ounce pike fillets
Pinch celery salt
1 tablespoon sweet butter
2 tablespoons water

Garnish: Celery Julienne (page 196)

Put 1½ cups celery in a saucepan and cover with water. Cook over medium-high heat until liquid is reduced by three-fourths. Strain the mixture through a fine mesh strainer, pressing on the solids to extract all the liquid. Put the remaining celery through a juice extractor. You should have 1½ cups of juice.

Whip 2 tablespoons cream until thick; set aside. Combine ½ cup of the strained celery reduction with the remaining ¼ cup cream in a saucepan. Cook over medium-high heat until reduced by three-fourths.

Season the pike fillets with celery salt. Arrange them in a single layer in a pan with the butter and water and cook over low heat for 4 minutes. Turn the fillets over and cook for 2 minutes longer.

Combine the raw celery juice with the celery-cream mixture and bring to a boil. Add the whipped cream and a pinch of celery salt. Bring to a boil.

Transfer the fish to warmed serving plates. Top with fried celery and pour the sauce around each serving of fish.

SERVES 4

COD WITH PINK RADISH JUICE

Cod is, to my taste, the finest American fish. It is harvested off the northeastern coast and is so plentiful that Portuguese fishermen travel the Atlantic to fish near our shores. Cod is not to be confused with Boston scrod, which is simply baby cod. Cod is thicker, and more subtle in its flavor and texture.

Prepare the radish juice at the very last moment. It will discolor if made ahead of time.

> *2 pounds radishes (5 cups)*
> *4 tablespoons sweet butter*
> *4 seven-ounce cod fillets*
> *Salt and cayenne pepper to taste*
> *2 tablespoons chopped chervil or radish greens*

Slice 1 cup of the radishes into very thin coins. Blanch them for 20 seconds in boiling salted water. Quickly refresh them under cold running water. Drain and set aside.

Melt 2 tablespoons butter in a medium sauté pan over medium-high heat. Add the fish and sauté 3 minutes per side. Remove and dry lightly with paper toweling. Season with salt and pepper. Put the remaining radishes through a juice extractor. You should have 2 cups of juice. (Do not juice the radishes ahead of time.) Bring the radish juice to a boil over medium-low heat and whisk in the remaining butter. Season with salt and cayenne pepper and add the chervil. Divide the sauce among 4 soup plates. Center a fillet in each plate and arrange radish coins over the fish to look like fish scales.

SERVES 4

BLACK BASS WITH BEET JUICE AND CAVIAR

Black bass is one of the most refined white-fleshed fishes. I don't season the fillets, just the sauce, and the naturally sharp flavor of the caviar adds a note of its own. The subtlety of the bass and caviar is balanced perfectly by the sweetness of the beet juice.

You can use any type of black caviar you wish. I advise against beluga, though, as it should be reserved for special occasions where it can be enjoyed without any accompaniment.

> 5 medium beets, peeled and chopped
> 1 tablespoon fresh lime juice
> 4 tablespoons sweet butter
> Salt and freshly ground pepper to taste
> 2 teaspoons chopped chives
> 4 seven-ounce black bass fillets
> 2 ounces caviar
>
> Garnish: Beet Chips (page 196)

Put the cut-up beets through a juice extractor. You should have 1¼ cups of juice.

In a small saucepan, heat the juice over medium-high heat until boiling. Reduce it by half. Add the lime juice and whisk in 3 tablespoons butter. Bring just to a boil and remove from heat. Season with salt and pepper. Add the chives.

Arrange the fillets in a single layer in a pan with enough water to reach halfway up the fish. Add the remaining 2 tablespoons butter and cook over low heat for 4 minutes. Turn the fillets over and cook for 2 minutes longer. Carefully drain the fillets and dry lightly with paper toweling.

Place the fish on warmed serving plates. Top with caviar and Beet Chips. Spoon some of the sauce around each serving of fish.

SERVES 4

Black Bass with Beet Juice and Caviar

CRAB CAKES WITH BROCCOLI JUICE

The natural starch in potato binds the cod cakes on page 58. Here, egg yolk binds the moist pieces of crab together. You can use ordinary mayonnaise if you don't have time to prepare the shellfish oil.

> 1 egg yolk
> ½ cup Lobster Oil (page 49) or Shrimp Oil (page 50)
> 1 pound crabmeat, picked over for cartilage
> 1 tablespoon chopped tarragon
> Salt and cayenne pepper to taste
> 2 cups unseasoned breadcrumbs, fresh or commercial
> 2 heads broccoli, 4 florets reserved for garnish
> 5 tablespoons sweet butter
> 1 teaspoon fresh lemon juice
> ¼ teaspoon sugar

In a medium bowl, lightly whisk the egg yolk. Add the Lobster Oil in a thin stream, whisking constantly until the mixture thickens to the consistency of mayonnaise. Add the crabmeat, tarragon, salt and cayenne pepper and mix well. Shape the mixture into small cakes, 2 inches in diameter. Coat them with breadcrumbs. Cover and refrigerate for 1 hour.

Put the broccoli through a juice extractor. You should have 2 cups of juice. In a small saucepan, heat the broccoli juice over medium-low heat. Whisk in 3 tablespoons butter, lemon juice, sugar, salt and cayenne pepper. Bring to a boil and remove from heat. Keep warm. Blanch the reserved florets in boiling salted water. Drain and immediately refresh under cold running water. Drain and set aside.

In a large sauté pan, melt the remaining 2 tablespoons butter over medium heat. Add the crab cakes and sauté until golden brown on both sides, about 3 minutes per side. Divide the crab cakes among warmed serving plates and pour some of the sauce around them. Garnish with the broccoli florets.

SERVES 4

SEA SCALLOPS WITH ZUCCHINI JUICE

This was one of my first vegetable juice recipes. It is a light version of a Provençal dish traditionally made with zucchini, garlic, thyme and browned butter in the place of olive oil. A serving of four scallops, rather than eight, makes an ample appetizer.

> 4 large zucchini, washed but not peeled, cut into chunks
> 3 tablespoons extra virgin olive oil
> ¼ teaspoon minced garlic
> ¼ teaspoon whole thyme leaves plus 4 sprigs thyme for garnish
> Salt and cayenne pepper to taste
> 32 large sea scallops, 4 shells reserved if possible

Put the zucchini through a juice extractor. You should have 2 cups of juice. Set aside.

In a saucepan, heat 1 tablespoon olive oil until hot. Add the garlic and sauté over medium heat until translucent. Reduce the heat to medium-low and add the zucchini juice and thyme leaves. Bring to a boil and remove from heat. Whisk in the remaining 2 tablespoons olive oil. Season with salt and cayenne pepper. Keep warm.

Heat a nonstick pan over medium-high heat. When it is hot, add the scallops and sauté 20 seconds per side. Season with salt and cayenne pepper.

If serving the scallops in shells, pour a small mound of salt in the center of each serving plate to anchor each shell. Put 8 scallops into each shell (or shallow soup plate). Pour the sauce over the scallops. Garnish with thyme sprigs.

SERVES 4

SEA SCALLOPS IN LEEK JUICE

This leek "juice" isn't extracted; it would be very sharp. Instead, the leeks are briefly cooked, then puréed.

> ½ medium leek, chopped, including some of
>   the green (1 cup)*
> 4 tablespoons sweet butter
> Salt and freshly ground pepper to taste
> 1 pound fresh wild mushrooms (chanterelles
>   or morels)
> 32 large sea scallops
>
> Garnish: 4 Leek Baskets (page 197)

Cook the leeks in 1 cup boiling salted water until tender, about 3 minutes. Drain leeks and reserve cooking liquid. Put the leeks in a blender with 1 tablespoon butter and blend until smooth. Put the leek purée and ½ cup of the cooking liquid in a clean saucepan. Season with salt and pepper. Keep warm.

Clean and quarter the mushrooms. In a large sauté pan, melt 1 tablespoon butter over medium-high heat. Add the mushrooms and sauté until their liquid evaporates. Season with salt and pepper.

In another pan, melt the remaining 2 tablespoons butter over medium-high heat. Add the scallops and sauté 20 seconds per side. Divide the scallops among warmed serving plates. Pour some sauce around the scallops. Put the sautéed mushrooms in each leek basket and place next to scallops.

SERVES 4

*Wash leeks very thoroughly before cooking them. To help rid them of sand, trim the root end from each and then cut 2 deep crosswise slits. Rinse under cold running water.

SHRIMP IN SPICY CARROT JUICE

The shrimp may be steamed (page 104) rather than sautéed, if you prefer. The seasoning has the same subtle piquancy of a spiced carrot cake; for a livelier version, add 1 teaspoon good-quality curry powder to the sauce. Remember, if the sauce starts to separate, whisk it over a low flame and it will come together again.

32 large shrimp (about 2 pounds)
10 medium carrots, peeled
A pinch each of ground cinnamon, ground
*   clove, ground nutmeg, salt and cayenne*
*   pepper*
1 teaspoon fresh lemon juice
6 tablespoons sweet butter
2 tablespoons chopped chervil

Garnish: Carrot Julienne (page 196)

Put the carrots through a juice extractor. You should have 2 cups of juice. Peel and devein shrimp, leaving the tails intact.

In a saucepan, combine the carrot juice, spices and lemon juice. Whisk in 4 tablespoons butter. Bring to a boil and remove from heat. Keep warm.

In a large sauté pan, melt the remaining 2 tablespoons butter over medium-high heat. Add the shrimp and sauté 1½ minutes per side until thoroughly pink. Season with salt and cayenne pepper.

Arrange 8 shrimp in each of 4 soup plates and pour sauce over them. Garnish with a little chopped chervil and Carrot Julienne.

SERVES 4

LOBSTER WITH ASPARAGUS JUICE

This dish contrasts sea and earth. Asparagus has great natural acidity, and the color and flavor of the juice perfectly complement the richness of lobster.

> 1½ pounds asparagus, trimmed but not
>   peeled
> 4 one-and-a-half-pound lobsters
> 4 asparagus spears, trimmed and peeled
> 6 tablespoons sweet butter
> Salt and cayenne pepper to taste
>
> Garnish: Asparagus Peelings (page 197)

Put the unpeeled asparagus through a juice extractor. You should have 1 cup of juice.

Blanch the lobsters in boiling salted water for 2 minutes; drain. Remove the meat from the tails and claws. Cut each tail into 5 medallions. Set aside.

Cook the asparagus spears in boiling salted water just until tender. Using the asparagus like brochettes, thread 5 lobster medallions on each spear. In a large sauté pan, melt 2 tablespoons butter over medium-high heat. Add the brochettes and claws and sauté for 2 minutes. Season with salt and cayenne pepper.

In a medium saucepan, combine the asparagus juice, the remaining 4 tablespoons butter, salt and cayenne pepper over medium-low heat. Bring to a boil, then remove from the heat. Keep warm.

Arrange 1 lobster brochette and 2 claws on each of 4 warmed serving plates. Pour the sauce around the lobster and garnish with Asparagus Peelings.

SERVES 4

LAMB CANNELLONI WITH ZUCCHINI JUICE

1 medium eggplant

¾ cup extra virgin olive oil

½ green bell pepper, seeded, deribbed and diced

½ red bell pepper, seeded, deribbed and diced

2 anchovies, chopped

2 medium button mushrooms, diced

¼ teaspoon minced garlic

Salt and freshly ground pepper to taste

2 racks of lamb, loins removed and trimmings saved (total weight of loins about 1 pound)

4 spring roll or egg roll wrappers*

3 medium zucchini, unpeeled, cut into chunks

1 tablespoon whole thyme leaves

2 tablespoons freshly grated Parmesan cheese

Heat the oven to 550 degrees. Roast the eggplant whole with olive oil for ½ hour. Remove from oven and reserve oil. (Leave the oven on.) Cut in half and scrape the flesh into a bowl; discard skin. Sauté the peppers, anchovies, mushrooms and garlic in 1 tablespoon reserved oil until soft. Add the eggplant, salt and pepper. Cook over medium-high heat for 10 minutes.

Chop the lamb trimmings. Sauté in 2 tablespoons reserved oil until golden and season with salt and pepper. Add to the eggplant mixture.

Cook the spring roll wrappers in boiling salted water until soft, about 15 seconds. Drain on paper toweling. Place 1½ to 2 tablespoons of the eggplant mixture on each wrapper. Roll the wrappers around the filling into cannelloni shapes.

Put the zucchini through a juice extractor. You should have 1 cup of juice. In a saucepan, combine the zucchini juice with 6 tablespoons reserved oil and thyme leaves. Bring to a boil and remove from heat. Keep warm.

In a medium sauté pan, heat 2 tablespoons reserved oil over medium-high heat until hot. Add the lamb loins and sauté until brown on both sides, about 1 minute per side. Remove the lamb to an ovenproof dish and finish cooking in the oven for 6 minutes.

Sprinkle the cannelloni with the cheese and put them under a preheated broiler until the cheese melts and is golden brown.

Season the lamb with salt and pepper and slice it. Divide the lamb and cannelloni among 4 warmed serving plates. Spoon some sauce around the lamb.

SERVES 4

*Spring roll and egg roll wrappers are available in Oriental markets. The spring roll cannelloni are lighter than those made conventionally with pasta. If you wish, follow the directions on page 135 to use rice paper rather than spring roll wrappers.

VEAL WITH CELERY JUICE AND ROQUEFORT CHEESE

Celery and Roquefort are a classic marriage that perfectly complements the subtle flavor of veal. For sautés I recommend seasoning meat only after it has cooked, but roasting is a different story.

> *4 tablespoons sweet butter*
> *2 tablespoons crumbled Roquefort cheese*
> *1 bunch celery, cut into pieces*
> *30-ounce saddle of veal*
> *Salt and freshly ground pepper to taste*
> *2 cups whole chanterelles or quartered*
>   *shiitake mushrooms, washed*
>   *thoroughly*
> *2 tablespoons chopped chives*
> *Celery salt to taste*
>
> *Garnish: Celeriac Chips (page 196)*
>   *Celery Leaves (page 196)*

Heat the oven to 500 degrees. Combine 3 tablespoons butter and the Roquefort in a food processor or blender. Process until smooth. (If preparing in advance, refrigerate until ready to use.)

Season the veal with salt and pepper. Put the veal in a roasting pan and roast for 15 minutes (for medium doneness).

Melt the remaining 1 tablespoon butter over medium-high heat. Add the mushrooms and sauté until their liquid evaporates. Season with salt and pepper and keep warm.

Put the celery through a juice extractor. You should have about 2 cups of juice. Put the celery juice in a saucepan and bring to a boil. Remove it from the heat and whisk in the Roquefort mixture. Add the chives and season with celery salt.

Slice the veal and arrange it on warmed serving plates with the mushrooms. Pour the sauce around the meat and garnish with Celeriac Chips and Celery Leaves.

SERVES 4

CHICKEN IN PINEAPPLE JUICE

This is an exotic dish, reminiscent of the Caribbean. Pineapple can be juiced just like any vegetable; the citrus attachment isn't necessary.

1 small pineapple, peeled
1 tablespoon freshly grated ginger
1 tablespoon orange marmalade
4 tablespoons sweet butter
¼ cup fresh lemon juice
3 tablespoons pine nuts
Salt and cayenne pepper to taste
4 whole chicken breasts, halved, skinned and boned

Put about half of the pineapple through a juice extractor. You should have 1 cup of juice.

Combine the pineapple juice, ginger and marmalade in a small, nonreactive saucepan. Bring to a boil over medium-high heat and reduce by half. Remove from heat and whisk in 2 tablespoons butter and the lemon juice. Add the pine nuts and season with salt and cayenne pepper. Set aside and keep warm.

Melt the remaining 2 tablespoons butter in a large sauté pan over medium-high heat. Add the chicken and sauté 3 minutes per side. Season with salt and cayenne pepper. Divide the chicken among 4 warmed serving plates and spoon some of the sauce over the chicken.

SERVES 4

BUILDING BLOCK: VINAIGRETTES

■

I began to learn about vinaigrettes in the first year of my apprenticeship at L'Auberge de l'Ill. The essence of any vinaigrette is to combine:

ONE PART ACID (VINEGAR, LEMON JUICE, LIME JUICE) TO TWO PARTS OIL

In order to make a vinaigrette lighter, I combine the ingredients in a food processor or blender to create an emulsion—the oil evenly distributed in tiny droplets throughout the mixture—and add a small amount of hot water to bind the vinaigrette further. These two extra steps make the vinaigrette lighter and even more flavorful than if it had simply been whisked.

■

BASIC VINAIGRETTE 1

The simplest of vinaigrettes is made by combining lemon juice and olive oil.

Put 2 tablespoons fresh lemon juice (the juice of 1 lemon) in a small food processor or blender with a pinch each of salt and freshly ground pepper.

Add ¼ cup extra virgin olive oil and process for 30 seconds.

Add 1½ teaspoons boiling water. Process again for 10 seconds. Serve immediately or store in a tightly covered jar or bottle in the refrigerator.

■

BASIC VINAIGRETTE 2

Put 2 tablespoons white wine vinegar, red wine vinegar or Champagne vinegar in a small food processor or blender with a pinch each of salt and freshly ground pepper.

Salmon in Rice Paper with Citrus Vinaigrette (page 23) garnished with potato "grid" (page 183). Vinaigrettes, in bottles, *from left to right:* Ginger, Soy and Ginger, Basic Vinaigrette 1, Peanut, Lobster, Sherry and Basil Vinaigrette.

Add ¼ cup canola or hazelnut oil and process for 30 seconds.

Add 1½ teaspoons boiling water. Process again for 10 seconds. Serve immediately or store in a tightly covered jar or bottle in the refrigerator.

Each vinaigrette, including most of those that follow, will keep in the refrigerator for 1 week, but as always—the fresher, the better. Each of the basic vinaigrettes is perfect on any form of salad. Use 2 tablespoons vinaigrette per serving on salads, 2 to 3 tablespoons to dress simple steamed or sautéed dishes.

The recipes that follow use the concepts just explained. Use these vinaigrettes instead of heavy or complicated sauces to accompany simply cooked meats, fish and shellfish.

GINGER VINAIGRETTE

½ cup extra virgin olive oil
1 tablespoon fresh lime juice
1 tablespoon sherry vinegar
1 teaspoon freshly grated ginger
Salt and freshly ground pepper to taste
1 tablespoon boiling water

Combine all ingredients except boiling water in a food processor or blender. Process for 30 seconds. With the motor running, add the water and process for 10 seconds longer. Store, tightly covered, in the refrigerator up to 1 day.

MAKES ¾ CUP

■

SOY AND GINGER VINAIGRETTE

½ cup soy sauce
½ cup fresh lemon juice
1 tablespoon freshly grated ginger
1½ cups extra virgin olive oil
1½ cups canola oil
Salt and freshly ground pepper to taste
6 tablespoons boiling water

Combine all ingredients except boiling water in a food processor or blender. Process for 30 seconds. With the motor running, add the water and process for 10 seconds longer. Store, tightly covered, in the refrigerator up to 1 week.

MAKES 4 CUPS

BASIL VINAIGRETTE

1 cup extra virgin olive oil
1 tablespoon fresh lemon juice
1 tablespoon sherry vinegar
12 large basil leaves
Salt and freshly ground pepper to taste
2 tablespoons boiling water

Combine all ingredients except boiling water in a food processor or blender. Process for 1 minute. With the motor running, add the water and process for 10 seconds longer. Store, tightly covered, in the refrigerator 1 day.

MAKES 1½ CUPS

NOTE: After 1 day, Basil Vinaigrette loses its pretty, clear green color. The flavor, though, will still be very nice for several days.

CITRUS VINAIGRETTE

½ cup extra virgin olive oil
1 tablespoon sherry vinegar
3 tablespoons soy sauce
Pinch cayenne pepper
2 pinches celery salt
1 drop tabasco
2 tablespoons boiling water
½ lime
1 lemon
¼ pink grapefruit
½ orange
10 pink peppercorns
1 tablespoon fresh ginger julienne
1 bunch cilantro, stems discarded and leaves cut into ribbons
Salt and freshly ground pepper to taste

Combine the oil, vinegar, soy sauce, cayenne pepper, celery salt and tabasco in a food processor or blender. Process for 30 seconds. With the motor running, add the water and process for 30 seconds longer. Transfer the mixture to a bowl and set aside.

Peel the fruits and remove the sections. Cut into small dice (reserve the juice).

Add the diced fruit to the bowl of vinaigrette with a teaspoon of each juice. Stir in the peppercorns, ginger and cilantro. Adjust seasoning with salt and pepper. Store, tightly covered, in the refrigerator up to 1 day. Or, prepare the vinaigrette base up to 1 week in advance and add the fruits, peppercorns, ginger and cilantro just before serving.

MAKES 1½ CUPS

CURRY VINAIGRETTE

½ cup Curry Oil (page 44)
½ cup sherry vinegar
Salt and freshly ground pepper to taste
1 tablespoon boiling water
½ medium apple, peeled and diced
½ medium banana, diced

Combine the oil, vinegar, salt and pepper in a food processor or blender. Process for 30 seconds. With the motor running, add the water and process for 10 seconds longer. Transfer the mixture to a bowl and stir in the diced apple and banana. Store, tightly covered, in the refrigerator up to 1 day. Or, prepare the vinaigrette base up to 1 week in advance and add the chopped apple and banana just before serving.

MAKES 2 CUPS

HAZELNUT VINAIGRETTE

2 tablespoons hazelnut oil
2 tablespoons canola oil
2 tablespoons sherry vinegar
1½ teaspoons boiling water
1 shallot, peeled and chopped
1 leek, white part only, washed thoroughly
   and chopped
Salt and freshly ground pepper to taste

Combine the oils and vinegar in a food processor or blender. Process for 30 seconds. With the motor running, add the water and process for 10 seconds longer. In a mixing bowl, combine shallot and leek. Add the vinaigrette and mix well. Season with salt and pepper. Store, tightly covered, in the refrigerator up to 1 week.

MAKES ½ CUP

JUNIPER VINAIGRETTE

1 tablespoon juniper berries
1 shallot, peeled and chopped
2 tablespoons sherry vinegar
1 tablespoon gin
2 tablespoons canola oil
2 tablespoons walnut oil
Salt and freshly ground pepper to taste
1½ teaspoons boiling water
1 bunch chives, chopped

Combine all ingredients except boiling water and chives in a food processor or blender. Process for 30 seconds. With the motor running, add the water and process for 1 minute longer. Stir in the chives. Store, tightly covered, in the refrigerator for up to 1 week

MAKES 1 CUP

PEANUT VINAIGRETTE

1 cup peanut oil*
¾ cup canola oil
¾ cup sherry vinegar
1 small leek, white part only, washed
    thoroughly and chopped
2 small shallots, peeled and chopped
Salt and freshly ground pepper to taste
3½ tablespoons boiling water

Combine all ingredients except boiling water in a food processor or blender. Process for 30 seconds. With the motor running, add the water and process for 10 seconds longer. Store, tightly covered, in the refrigerator up to 1 week.

MAKES 2½ CUPS

*If you can find oil pressed from roasted peanuts, by all means use it. It is darker in color than oil from unroasted peanuts and has a more pronounced peanut flavor.

TRUFFLE VINAIGRETTE

1 cup canola oil
2 tablespoons fresh lemon juice
1 tablespoon sherry vinegar
3 tablespoons truffle juice*
Salt and freshly ground pepper to taste
2 tablespoons boiling water

Combine all ingredients except boiling water in a food processor or blender. Process for 30 seconds. With the motor running, add the water and process for 1 minute longer. Store, tightly covered, in the refrigerator 1 week.

MAKES 1½ CUPS

*Truffle juice can be purchased in cans in specialty stores and gourmet markets. As you can see, a little goes a long way. You may also use the liquid in which jarred or canned truffles are packed.

LOBSTER OR SHRIMP VINAIGRETTE

2 tablespoons Champagne or white wine vinegar
¼ cup Lobster Oil (page 49) or Shrimp Oil (page 50)
1 tablespoon Dijon mustard
¼ cup fresh lemon juice
Salt and freshly ground pepper to taste
1½ teaspoons boiling water
2 tablespoons capers
2 tablespoons chives cut into ½-inch lengths

Combine all ingredients except boiling water, capers and chives in a food processor or blender. Process for 30 seconds. With the motor running, add the water and process for 1 minute longer. Stir in the capers and chives just before serving. Store, tightly covered, in the refrigerator up to 1 week.

MAKES 1 CUP

SALMON IN RICE PAPER WITH CITRUS VINAIGRETTE

Several sprigs flat-leaf parsley
4 six-ounce skinless salmon fillets (about 3 ×
*   1½ × 1 inch)*
4 eight-inch sheets rice paper
1 tablespoon canola oil
1 tablespoon sweet butter
½ cup Citrus Vinaigrette (page 19)

Heat the oven to 425 degrees. Press 2 or 3 parsley leaves onto one side of each fillet.

Soften each round of rice paper between layers of damp kitchen toweling for about 5 minutes until pliable enough to roll without cracking but not wet.

Wrap each fillet in rice paper: Place it about 2 inches from the bottom of the circle. Bring the bottom over the fillet, then roll the fillet to enclose it. Trim the sides off until even with the salmon.

In a medium nonstick pan, heat the oil and butter over medium-high heat until hot. Add the salmon packages and sauté 1½ minutes per side until rice paper is crisp. Transfer to an ovenproof dish, put in the oven and cook for 2 minutes. Remove from the oven, cover and let rest for 1 minute.

Slice each package into 3 pieces. Arrange the slices on warmed serving plates. Serve with Citrus Vinaigrette.

SERVES 4

BUCKWHEAT PASTA WITH BLACK BASS AND CAVIAR

This recipe is inspired by the famous Russian dish of buckwheat blini with sturgeon and caviar. The buckwheat pasta is quite easy, but if you don't want to make it yourself, buy fresh pasta. In a pinch, boxed dried lasagne noodles will do nicely. This is a very festive dish for a special occasion.

Buckwheat Pasta (right)
3 tablespoons sweet butter
1 shallot, peeled and chopped
1 cup dry white wine
1 cup Mixed Vegetable Broth (page 75)
1 cup heavy cream
½ cucumber, finely julienned
4 large white button mushrooms, finely julienned
Salt and freshly ground pepper to taste
1 pound black bass fillets, cut into 2 × 4-inch pieces
Caviar Vinaigrette (page 26)

Prepare the Buckwheat Pasta.

In a medium saucepan, melt 1 tablespoon butter over medium-high heat. Add the shallot and cook until translucent. Add the wine and cook until evaporated. Add the Mixed Vegetable Broth and reduce by half. Add the cream, cucumber and mushrooms. Season with salt and pepper. Cook until thickened. Keep warm.

Melt the remaining 2 tablespoons butter in a sauté pan. Arrange the pieces of fish in a single layer in the butter and cook over medium-high heat for 3 minutes. Turn the fish over and cook 3 minutes longer or until desired doneness.

Cook the pasta for 45 seconds to 1 minute in boiling salted water. Drain. Combine all the ingredients for the Caviar Vinaigrette and set it aside.

Fan 3 pieces of pasta alternately with 2 pieces of fish on each of 4 serving plates. Spoon some of the sauce over each and pour Caviar Vinaigrette around the fish.

SERVES 4

BUCKWHEAT PASTA

¾ cup buckwheat flour
Scant ½ cup all-purpose flour
1 egg
1 egg yolk
1 tablespoon extra virgin olive oil
1 tablespoon milk
Pinch of salt

Combine all ingredients by hand or in a food processor or blender to form a dough. Knead briefly. Cover and let rest in the refrigerator for at least ½ hour. Roll it out to ⅛-inch thickness with a rolling pin on a lightly floured surface or run it through a pasta machine. Cut the pasta into small rectangles, 2 × 4 inches. Cover with plastic wrap and refrigerate until needed.

Buckwheat Pasta with Black Bass and Caviar

CAVIAR VINAIGRETTE

2 tablespoons sherry vinegar
3 tablespoons safflower or grapeseed oil
2 tablespoons caviar (sevruga if possible)
Salt and freshly ground pepper to taste

Combine all ingredients and set aside.

■

SKATE WINGS WITH ARTICHOKES

Lobster or Shrimp Vinaigrette, together with the artichokes, provides just the right amount of acidity to balance skate, one of the more gelatinous or fatty fishes. If you are pressed for time, you may use frozen (thawed) artichoke hearts here.

8 medium artichokes
2 tablespoons fresh lemon juice
3 tablespoons extra virgin olive oil
1 medium onion, peeled and sliced
2 cups dry white wine
Salt and freshly ground pepper to taste
Canola oil, for frying
1 tablespoon all-purpose flour
2 tablespoons sweet butter
1 pound skate wing fillets
½ cup Lobster or Shrimp Vinaigrette
   (page 22)

Trim artichoke hearts as directed on page 76. Put the hearts in a bowl of water acidulated with lemon juice (to keep them from discoloring).

Heat the olive oil in a nonreactive saucepan and sauté the onion until translucent. Add 6 of the artichoke hearts and the wine. Cook over medium heat until hearts are tender. Put the hearts in a food processor or blender with 2 tablespoons cooking liquid and process to a smooth purée. Season with salt and pepper and set aside.

Heat the canola oil (1 inch deep) until very hot (350 to 375 degrees). Drain the 2 remaining artichoke hearts and pat dry. Cut them into matchstick pieces. Flour them lightly and fry until golden brown and crisp. Drain on paper toweling and salt lightly.

Heat the butter in a sauté pan. Add the skate and cook over medium-high heat 20 seconds per side. Season with salt and pepper.

Place the skate on warmed serving plates. Spoon some artichoke purée down the center of each fillet and top with the fried artichoke matchsticks. Pour some Lobster or Shrimp Vinaigrette around the skate.

SERVES 4

SALMON CABBAGE WITH JUNIPER VINAIGRETTE

This is my version of the classic stuffed cabbage. The juniper berry is very pungent and goes extremely well with cabbage.

You can prepare the salmon and cabbage rolls in the morning or even the night before, then slice and sauté them at the last minute.

> 1 savoy cabbage (or any other cabbage if savoy is unavailable)
> 1½ pounds salmon fillets, sliced ⅓ inch thick
> 2 tablespoons canola oil
> ½ cup Juniper Vinaigrette (page 21)
>
> Garnish: 12 Gaufrette Potatoes (page 55), homemade potato chips, or even good-quality potato chips straight from the bag
> 12 stalks chives, cut into 2-inch lengths
> 2 tablespoons salmon roe

Core the cabbage and carefully separate the leaves. Blanch the leaves for 1 minute in boiling salted water. Quickly refresh them in a bowl of ice water. Drain and pat dry.

Lay a piece of aluminum foil approximately 8 × 10 inches on a work surface. Cover the foil with cabbage leaves. Cover cabbage completely with salmon. Lift the edge of the foil on the long side and, with a spatula, roll cabbage and salmon into a tight cylinder. Roll tightly in the foil. Twist the ends of the foil tightly. Refrigerate for at least 2 hours.

Unwrap the rolled salmon and cut into 1-inch slices. Heat canola oil in a sauté pan and cook the slices over medium-high heat 30 seconds per side.

Arrange 3 slices on each of 4 serving plates. Sprinkle with Juniper Vinaigrette and garnish with Gaufrette Potatoes, chives and roe.

SERVES 4

Following Pages: Skate Wings with Artichokes, Salmon Cabbage with Juniper Vinaigrette, garnished with fried artichokes and Gaufrette Potatoes (page 55).

SALAD OF CRAYFISH, ZUCCHINI AND TOMATO

This is a fresh salad without lettuce. Shrimp works just as well as crayfish, is less expensive and more plentiful. If you can find crayfish from New Orleans or the West Coast, by all means try them.

> 48 whole crayfish or , 24 medium shrimp, peeled and deveined
> 2 medium zucchini
> 2 tablespoons extra virgin olive oil
> 1 medium onion, peeled and chopped
> 2 cloves garlic, peeled and chopped
> 4 medium tomatoes, peeled, seeded and coarsely chopped
> ½ bunch fresh thyme, tied into a bundle with kitchen string
> Salt and freshly ground pepper to taste
> ½ cup Basil Vinaigrette (page 19)
>
> Garnish: 4 sprigs basil

Following the directions on page 104 for shrimp, steam the crayfish for 5 minutes, then let cool. Separate the tails from the bodies. Remove the tail meat and discard the shells and bodies. (If using shrimp, steam as directed on page 104 for 5 minutes; set aside.)

Slice the zucchini into thin coins and blanch them in boiling salted water for 1 minute. Drain and refresh under cold running water.

Heat the olive oil over medium-high heat and sauté the onion and garlic until translucent. Add the tomatoes and thyme and cook for 15 minutes, stirring occasionally. Remove and discard the thyme. Set the mixture aside to cool.

Season the zucchini, crayfish and tomatoes individually with salt and pepper. Pour the Basil Vinaigrette over the tomatoes and stir well.

On each of 4 serving plates, overlap zucchini slices to form a large ring. Arrange crayfish within the rings. Spoon the tomato mixture around the zucchini and garnish with basil sprigs.

SERVES 4

COLD SEA URCHIN SOUFFLE

1 generous cup sea urchins*
1 cup Mixed Vegetable Broth (page 75)
2 egg yolks
½ teaspoon unflavored gelatin
1 cup heavy cream, whipped
¼ teaspoon fresh lemon juice
Salt and cayenne pepper to taste
½ cup Ginger Vinaigrette (page 18)

Press the sea urchins through a fine sieve to obtain a purée. In a medium saucepan, combine the sea urchin purée, Mixed Vegetable Broth and egg yolks. Heat gently over low heat, whisking constantly, until lukewarm. Sprinkle the gelatin over the mixture and cook, whisking constantly, until gelatin is dissolved and mixture is hot and slightly thickened. (Do not let the mixture boil, or the egg yolks will scramble.)

Transfer the mixture to a mixing bowl set in a larger bowl filled with ice water. Gently stir the mixture as it cools. When it is cool to the touch and has thickened, remove the bowl from the ice water and fold in the whipped cream. Season with lemon juice, salt and cayenne pepper.

Pour into espresso-size cups or 2-ounce ramekins. Cover tightly and refrigerate until set, at least 1 hour.

When ready to serve, unmold each soufflé by dipping the cup into hot water and running a knife around the inside of the cup. Invert onto a small serving plate. Serve with a drizzle of Ginger Vinaigrette.

SERVES 8

*Sea urchin (*uni* in Japanese) may be obtained at Japanese grocers, from some Japanese restaurants and some fishmongers. The distinctive flavor of sea urchin comes through most clearly when eaten cold and uncooked. This may be too much for the less adventuresome, so I created this dish which gentles the flavor with cooking, then cools to a soufflé. Serve these little soufflés with the wonderfully crisp Rice Crackers on page 162.

STEAMED SHRIMP WITH CHAMPAGNE VINAIGRETTE

This warm salad combines hot shrimp with cooling greens and a tangy Champagne vinaigrette. Warm salads eventually became popular in France, but it seems to me no one understood the marriage of such diverse elements better than my mentor, Louis Outhier, who always featured warm salads on his seasonal menu at L'Oasis in La Napoule.

> 3 tablespoons sweet butter
> 1 medium shallot, peeled and finely chopped
> ½ cup Champagne or white wine vinegar
> ½ cup heavy cream
> Salt and cayenne pepper to taste
> 24 large shrimp, peeled and deveined
> 2 cups mixed salad greens
> 1 medium avocado
> 4 medium button mushrooms, caps very thinly
>   sliced and stems julienned
> 1 medium tomato, peeled, seeded and diced
> ½ cup Soy and Ginger Vinaigrette (page 18)

In a medium saucepan, melt 1 tablespoon butter over medium-high heat and sauté the shallot until translucent. Add the vinegar and cook until reduced by half. Add the cream and cook until reduced by half. Whisk in the remaining 2 tablespoons butter, bring to a boil and immediately remove from heat. Season with salt and cayenne pepper and keep warm.

Steam the shrimp as directed on page 104 until they are pink throughout, 3 to 4 minutes. Season with salt and cayenne pepper.

While the shrimp are cooking, arrange the greens on each of 4 serving plates. Peel and cut the avocado into thin slices. Place 2 or 3 slices of avocado on the greens on each plate. Scatter mushrooms over them and top with a small spoonful of diced tomato. Drizzle with 2 tablespoons Soy and Ginger Vinaigrette. Arrange the shrimp around the greens and spoon some of the Champagne vinegar sauce over them.

SERVES 4

OPEN RAVIOLI WITH SHRIMP

Reminiscent of lasagne, this dish is more precisely known as "open ravioli." It always struck me that shrimp, lobster, scallops and other delicate ravioli fillings frequently overcook, as the boiling of the pasta controls the cooking of the filling. Here, the pasta and the shrimp are cooked separately.

There is no limit to the different fillings you can use. Let your imagination know no bounds. If you don't want to make your own pasta, trim fresh or cooked, dried lasagne noodles.

> 5 tablespoons sweet butter
> 24 large shrimp, peeled and deveined
> 2 medium shallots, peeled and chopped
> 1 clove garlic, peeled and chopped
> 1 cup dry white wine
> 2 tablespoons chopped parsley
> Salt and freshly ground pepper to taste
> Pasta (right), prepared 1 day in advance
> ½ cup Lobster or Shrimp Vinaigrette
>   (page 22)

In a large sauté pan, melt 3 tablespoons butter over medium-high heat and sauté the shrimp for 1 minute on each side. Add the shallots and garlic and cook for about 20 seconds. Deglaze the pan with the wine. Remove the shrimp from the pan and keep warm. Reduce the liquid in the pan by one-third. Whisk in the remaining 2 tablespoons butter. Add the parsley and shrimp and season with salt and pepper. Set aside and keep warm.

Cook the pasta in boiling salted water for 15 seconds. Drain immediately and lightly pat dry.

Place one unmarked sheet of pasta on each of 4 serving plates. Put 6 shrimp and some sauce on each square of pasta, then cover with a sheet of "parsley printed" pasta. Sprinkle Lobster Vinaigrette around the plate.

SERVES 4

PASTA

> 2 cups all-purpose flour
> 3 eggs
> 1 teaspoon white wine vinegar
> Pinch salt
> 4 flat-leaf parsley leaves

Mix the flour, eggs, vinegar and salt in a food processor or by hand until very well combined. Cover and let rest in the refrigerator overnight. Roll out the pasta by hand or use a pasta machine until paper thin. Cut out eight 2-inch squares. Decorate 4 of the sheets with a parsley leaf, pressing the leaves into the dough so they adhere.

LOBSTER COUSCOUS

This is a memorable salad, served at room temperature. If you like, you can shape the couscous for each serving in individual savarin (ring) molds. Pack it down firmly, then turn it out. I would arrange lobster medallions in the center with a claw on either side.

1 medium carrot, chopped
½ medium leek, white part only, washed thoroughly and chopped
½ medium onion, chopped
1 stalk celery, chopped
1 Bouquet Garni (page 194)
Four 1-pound lobsters
¼ teaspoon harissa pepper or Chinese chili paste
⅔ cup extra virgin olive oil
1 cup couscous
4 mint leaves, cut into ribbons
4 basil leaves, cut into ribbons
2 medium tomatoes, peeled, seeded and chopped
1 medium cucumber, peeled, seeded and chopped
½ cup diced pitted ripe olives
Salt and freshly ground pepper to taste
1 cup Ginger Vinaigrette (page 18)
2 tablespoons chopped chervil

Add the carrot, leek, onion, celery and Bouquet Garni to a large pot of water and bring to a rolling boil. Add the lobsters and cook for 10 minutes.

Remove the lobsters from the broth. Strain and reserve 1¾ cups of the broth. Carefully remove the lobster meat; cut each tail into 5 medallions and leave the claws whole. Set aside in a large bowl.

Put the reserved broth in a medium saucepan with the harissa pepper and olive oil. Whisk over medium-high heat until hot. Pour over the couscous. Let the couscous sit for 20 minutes, without stirring, until it has absorbed all or nearly all of the liquid. Gently stir in the mint, basil, tomatoes, cucumber and olives.

Season the lobster with salt and pepper. Add enough Ginger Vinaigrette to coat, turning gently. Divide the couscous among 4 serving plates. Arrange 5 medallions and 2 claws on or around each serving. Drizzle each serving with 2 to 3 tablespoons Ginger Vinaigrette and scatter chervil over all.

SERVES 4

SQUAB AND LENTIL SALAD

This is a perfect fall and winter dish, one of my favorites. I always felt that this was a rich combination of metallic flavors: the "copper" of squab and the "iron" of lentils.

> 1 cup dried lentils
>
> 2 squab or 1 two- to three-pound baby chicken, skinned and boned
>
> ¼ cup cooked foie gras or chicken livers, diced
>
> 1 tablespoon sweet butter
>
> Salt and freshly ground pepper to taste
>
> ½ cup frisée lettuce (chicory)
>
> ¾ cup Peanut Vinaigrette (page 21)
>
> ½ cup Mushroom Syrup (page 74)
>
> 1 tablespoon sherry vinegar
>
> 2 tablespoons peanut oil
>
> 1 teaspoon cracked black peppercorns
>
> ¼ cup cracked raw peanuts

Soak the lentils in cold water for 2 hours. Drain, put into a pot and cover with salted water. Bring to a boil; reduce heat and simmer until tender, about 30 minutes. Drain and set aside.

Stuff the leg meat with the cooked foie gras. Roll each leg in a piece of aluminum foil. Put the foil packages in a pot of water and bring to a boil. Immediately remove the pot from the heat and let the packages cool in the water until ready to use.

Melt the butter over medium-high heat and sauté the breasts 2 minutes per side. Season with salt and pepper. Cut each breast into 4 slices.

Season the frisée lettuce with salt, pepper and ¼ cup of the vinaigrette. Season the lentils separately with salt, pepper and the remaining vinaigrette.

Warm the Mushroom Syrup and whisk in the vinegar and peanut oil.

Mound some of the frisée in the center of each serving plate. Spoon lentils on top of the frisée. Unwrap the stuffed legs and place one on each plate. Add slices of squab breast to each plate and sprinkle cracked black pepper and peanuts over all. Pour some of the mushroom sauce over the breast meat.

SERVES 4

SWEETBREADS WITH YELLOW POTATO SALAD

Potato salad with crisp bacon is a dish that I grew up with in Alsace. Here the potatoes dominate, and we add the crispness of sautéed sweetbreads. Blanching the sweetbreads before sautéing them guarantees they will be very crisp. Use a variety of salad greens, as fresh as you can find.

1 pound sweetbreads
4 medium yellow or red-skin potatoes
3 tablespoons duck fat or hazelnut oil
All-purpose flour
Salt and freshly ground pepper to taste
¾ cup Hazelnut Vinaigrette (page 20)
½ pound mixed salad greens

Blanch the sweetbreads in boiling salted water for 1 minute. Drain and let cool to room temperature. Place the cooled sweetbreads in a pan. Set another pan on top of them and weight it. Let the sweetbreads "press" for 30 minutes.

Cook the potatoes in boiling salted water until tender when pierced with a fork, about 15 minutes. Peel and slice ¼ inch thick.

Slice the sweetbreads on the diagonal about ½-inch thick. Flour them lightly. In a large sauté pan, heat the duck fat over medium-high heat until very hot. Sauté sweetbreads and potatoes on both sides until golden brown and crisp, about 4 minutes. Season with salt and pepper.

Toss sweetbreads and potatoes in Hazelnut Vinaigrette.

Divide the salad greens among 4 serving plates. Arrange a circle of potatoes on the greens with the sweetbreads in the center. Sprinkle more of the vinaigrette over all.

SERVES 4

Sweetbreads with Yellow Potato Salad

BEEF ON A STRING WITH BASIL VINAIGRETTE

This is my version of a fast *pot-au-feu*, or boiled dinner. Have your butcher cut the sirloin for you, very thin as for Japanese *sukiyaki*. If you follow the directions carefully, the vegetables will be crisp-tender and the meat moist and flavorful.

> 2 medium carrots, peeled
> 2 long turnips, peeled
> 2 medium zucchini
> 8 string beans, trimmed
> 8 pencil-thin stalks asparagus, trimmed and peeled
> 12 thin slices prime sirloin, about 5 × 1½ inches and no more than ¼ inch thick
> Salt and freshly ground pepper to taste
> 1 quart Vegetable Broth (right)
> Basil Vinaigrette with Vegetables (page 39)

Cut the carrots, turnips and zucchini into matchstick pieces about 2½ inches long. Cook the vegetables in boiling salted water until tender, zucchini 30 seconds, carrots, beans, turnips and asparagus 1½ to 2 minutes.

Lay sirloin slices on a flat surface. Season with salt and pepper. Divide vegetables among the meat slices and roll the meat around them. Secure each roll with kitchen string.

Heat the broth until boiling. Place the meat rolls in the broth and poach them for 40 seconds. Remove them immediately. Cut off the string. Serve with Basil Vinaigrette with Vegetables.

SERVES 4

VEGETABLE BROTH

> 1 tablespoon extra virgin olive oil
> 1 tablespoon sweet butter
> 1 medium carrot, peeled and diced
> 1 bulb fennel, diced
> 5 leeks, white part only, washed thoroughly and sliced
> 10 shallots, peeled and chopped
> 10 cloves garlic, peeled and chopped
> ¼ cup chopped chervil
> ½ cup chopped dill
> 2 cups dry white wine
> ¼ teaspoon cracked coriander seed
> ¼ teaspoon cracked black pepper
> 3½ cups water

In a medium pot, heat the olive oil and butter over medium-high heat. Add the vegetables and cook until soft. Add the herbs, wine, coriander seed and pepper. Cook until the wine evaporates. Add the water and cook for 20 minutes. Strain through a fine mesh strainer, pressing on the solids to extract as much liquid as possible.

BASIL VINAIGRETTE WITH VEGETABLES

Basil Vinaigrette (page 19)
½ medium red bell pepper, seeded, deribbed and finely diced
½ medium zucchini, finely diced
½ medium tomato, peeled, seeded and finely diced
1 clove garlic, peeled and finely chopped
2 shallots, peeled and finely chopped
½ teaspoon chopped chives
½ teaspoon chopped parsley
½ teaspoon chopped tarragon
½ teaspoon chopped dill

Combine all ingredients.

FRESH TRUFFLE SALAD

As you probably know, truffles are very expensive whether they be fresh, canned or jarred. I try never to use truffles unless they are fresh, in January or February. When fresh, their intensity is remarkable. This dish is a pure extravagance, but one that truly exploits the natural flavor of the truffle.

2 tablespoons fresh lemon juice
2 tablespoons extra virgin olive oil
Salt and freshly ground pepper to taste
½ pound mixed salad greens
1 knob celeriac, peeled and finely julienned
2 medium black truffles (fresh only), thinly shaved

Whisk together the lemon juice, olive oil, salt and pepper.

Place some greens on each of 4 plates. Dip the truffle slices into the olive oil dressing and arrange them in a ring around the greens. Scatter the celeriac over all and spoon some dressing over the salad.

SERVES 4

ASPARAGUS SALAD

This is a wonderful vegetarian salad for the spring and summer. The hot asparagus and cold salad are a nice contrast, what we call a *chaud-froid* in French.

> 1 pound asparagus, trimmed and peeled
> 1 medium avocado
> 1 tablespoon plus 1 teaspoon fresh lemon juice
> 2 egg yolks
> 6 tablespoons water
> 4 tablespoons sweet butter, softened
> Salt and cayenne pepper to taste
> 2 heads endive, leaves separated
> 1 pound mixed salad greens
> 2 three-ounce packages enoki mushrooms or 8 thinly sliced button mushrooms
> ½ cup Soy and Ginger Vinaigrette (page 18)
> 1 teaspoon chopped chives or parsley

Tie the asparagus in 3 bunches. Cook in boiling salted water until tender, about 5 minutes. Drain and immediately refresh under cold running water.

Peel and thinly slice the avocado. Gently toss with 1 tablespoon lemon juice and set aside.

In a double boiler set over simmering water, whisk together the egg yolks, a pinch of salt and the water until frothy.

Beat in the soft butter and whisk until thick enough to coat a spoon. Don't let the Hollandaise curdle. Season with salt, cayenne pepper and 1 teaspoon lemon juice.

Arrange 5 endive leaves on each of 4 serving plates to form a star. Place mixed greens in the center of each. Top with 3 slices of avocado and sprinkle with mushrooms. Dress with the vinaigrette. Top with the warm asparagus. Spoon 2 tablespoons Hollandaise over each portion of asparagus and sprinkle with chives or parsley.

SERVES 4

CHANTERELLES AND SPINACH SALAD

"Baby" spinach leaves are very tender, and their small size is so appealing. Wash and dry the mushrooms and spinach well.

   ¼ cup peanut oil
   1 clove garlic, peeled and chopped
   2 shallots, peeled and chopped
   1 pound chanterelles or shiitake mushrooms, washed thoroughly
   Salt and freshly ground pepper to taste
   ½ pound "baby" or regular spinach, stemmed and washed thoroughly
   ⅓ cup Hazelnut Vinaigrette (page 20)
   ¼ cup mixed chopped herbs (chervil, parsley and chives)
   ¼ cup hazelnut or extra virgin olive oil
   1 teaspoon soy sauce
   2 tablespoons water

In a medium sauté pan, heat the peanut oil over medium-high heat. When hot, add the garlic and shallots and cook until translucent. Add the mushrooms. Season with salt and pepper. Cover and cook for 12 minutes, stirring occasionally.

Lightly pat spinach dry and toss with Hazelnut Vinaigrette. Add the chopped herbs and toss. Arrange on plates.

Add hazelnut oil, soy sauce and water to the mushrooms. Cook, uncovered, until the cooking liquid is reduced by half. Arrange the mushrooms on the spinach and spoon over some of the sauce.

SERVES 4

BUILDING BLOCK: FLAVORED OILS

■

Like the vegetable juices and vinaigrettes, the flavored oils are "building blocks" in many of my recipes, and they too can be served with the quickly prepared sautés or steamed dishes of meat, poultry, fish and shellfish found on pages 93 to 105. With any of the flavored oils on hand, a memorable—and astonishingly simple—dinner can be made in minutes.

Flavored oils can be used in as many ways as you can imagine. They provide nearly infinite inspiration when you want to dress a salad (try a vinaigrette of Mustard Oil with sherry vinegar). They make for absolutely unheard-of mayonnaises. Use them in the place of butter or oil when sautéing. You could even, if you wished, deep-fat fry in a flavored oil.

I use the oils most often, I think, to drizzle over sautéed and steamed foods, for an effect as elegant as it is simple. Don't hesitate to moisten pieces of fresh, crusty bread with it. Finally, anytime you marinate meats before grilling them, consider marinating them in one of your flavored oils (see page 181). The flavor is incomparable.

All of the flavored oils may be prepared in advance. They are as delicious served cold as when gently heated.

There are various types of oils, prepared by slightly different methods. The techniques are so simple they can be mastered the first time you make them. Whenever I use a "neutral" oil, I prefer to use canola oil (which has the lowest saturated fat content).

GROUND SPICE OILS   FRESH ROOT OILS   VEGETABLE JUICE OILS   HERB OILS   FRUIT OILS

MISCELLANEOUS OILS

Rabbit Sausage with Mustard Oil (page 69), Red Snapper in Potato Flakes with Tomato Oil (page 60). Flavored oils, in bottles, *from left to right:* Mustard, Orange-Basil, Chive, Red Pepper, Curry, Cilantro, Orange, Lobster and Tomato Oil.

GROUND SPICE OILS

MUSTARD	GARLIC
PAPRIKA	CUMIN
CURRY	ANISE
TURMERIC	CINNAMON
GINGER	WASABI
CARAWAY	FENNEL
CARDAMOM	SAFFRON

Each spice is in powdered form.

To make a spiced oil, first mix water with the ground spice before the oil is added. This rejuvenates or "wakes up" the flavor of the spice. Without this first step, the essential flavor of the spice won't reach its potential.

If you can't find caraway, cardamom, anise or fennel in powdered form, you can grind the spices yourself in a clean electric coffee grinder, mortar and pestle or small ("mini") food processor.

METHOD

Mix 3 tablespoons ground spice with 1 table-spoon water to a smooth paste. If the paste is very dry, add a little more water. The paste should not be liquid; the consistency of ketchup is just about right.

Put the paste in a clear jar.

Add 2 cups of canola oil.

Cover the jar tightly and shake vigorously.

Set the jar on a kitchen shelf for 2 days. You may shake the oil several times during this time to increase the strength of the oil.

The spice particles will gradually settle to the bottom of the jar. After 2 days, remove the oil on top with a ladle, being careful not to disturb the solids at the bottom too much. Discard the solids. Filter the oil—not the solids—through a paper coffee filter or a double thickness of fine cheesecloth. Do not filter the solids!

Store the spiced oil, tightly covered, in the refrigerator or at room temperature for up to 6 months.

MAKES 2 CUPS

FRESH ROOT OILS

SHALLOT
GARLIC
HORSERADISH
GINGER
LEEK

These highly flavored fresh roots combine beautifully with oils. ("Root" is most evocative but not strictly accurate, for shallots and garlic are really bulbs, leeks are vegetables and ginger is a rhizome.) Since the flavorings are fresh, they don't need to be mixed with water; they will "wake up" when combined with oil. Due to the individual, characteristic flavor of each, some oils complement that flavor better than others.

Because the roots are pungent and fresh, the flavored oil will be ready to use just 1 to 2 hours after mixing. These oils must be kept tightly covered in the refrigerator, where they will keep up to 2 weeks.

METHOD

Peel the roots. If using leeks, quarter them lengthwise and rinse thoroughly of any sand; pat dry.

Mince the roots by hand or finely chop in a food processor. (If using a food processor, one of the small "mini" models is preferred. It is nearly impossible to process small amounts of garlic and the like to uniformly tiny pieces in the larger machines.)

For every 2 tablespoons of chopped root, add 2 cups of the appropriate oil:

SHALLOT	Canola oil
GARLIC	Extra virgin olive oil
HORSERADISH	Canola oil
GINGER	Canola oil
LEEK	Walnut or hazelnut oil

Put the chopped root in a clean jar. Add oil. Cover the jar tightly and shake vigorously.

Store the root oil, tightly covered, in the refrigerator for at least 1 to 2 hours.

MAKES 2 CUPS

VEGETABLE JUICE OILS

These oils combine freshly extracted vegetable juices with oils. Every one of the vegetable juice oils may be used as a delicious sauce by itself. Bell pepper juice and beet juice may be reduced to a syrup and then combined with oil for a sauce with especially brilliant flavor and color. Vegetable juice oils are ready to use immediately.

METHOD

Make 1 cup of the desired vegetable juice as described on page 1. Put the juice in a clear jar.

Add 2 cups of the appropriate oil. Combine the juices and oils as follows:

CARROT	Canola oil
ZUCCHINI	Extra virgin olive oil
ASPARAGUS	Canola oil
BELL PEPPER	Extra virgin olive oil
CELERY	Canola oil
BEET	Canola oil
LEEK	Canola oil

Cover the jar tightly and shake vigorously.

Store the vegetable juice oil, tightly covered, in the refrigerator for up to 2 weeks. For an oil with uniform color, shake well before using. I prefer not to, though, as the oil is so pretty when it is "broken," the tiny pieces of vegetable color catching the light. Never filter a vegetable juice oil.

MAKES 3 CUPS

HERB OILS

These oils are flavored with fresh herbs only. There are 2 types of herb oils, those made with tender, mild herbs and those made with stronger herbs.

TENDER, MILD HERBS

BASIL

CHERVIL

PARSLEY

CILANTRO

MINT

METHOD

Blanch the herbs (including their stems) in boiling water for 15 seconds. Quickly refresh them under cold running water. Drain and dry them well.

Measure the herbs and place in a blender. Add an equal amount of extra virgin olive oil.

Blend to a smooth paste. Remove to a clean bottle or jar and add 3 times as much olive oil as paste. Shake to combine thoroughly. Store for 1 day. When the herbs have settled, filter the oil through a paper coffee filter. The oil is ready to use.

Store, tightly covered, in the refrigerator for up to 1 week.

MAKES 3 CUPS

STRONGER HERBS

THYME

ROSEMARY

MARJORAM

OREGANO

METHOD

Separate the leaves from the stems; discard the stems. Mince the herbs by hand or in a small ("mini") food processor.

Mix 1 cup minced herb with 2 cups canola oil in a clean jar. Shake well. Let the oil sit at room temperature for 2 hours.

Store, tightly covered, in the refrigerator for up to 1 month.

MAKES 3 CUPS

FRUIT OILS

CRANBERRY
ORANGE
PINEAPPLE
PINK GRAPEFRUIT
POMEGRANATE

The clear, strong flavors of these fruits make delectable oils.

METHOD

Make 2 cups of juice from any of the fresh fruits above (commercially prepared cranberry, orange and pineapple juices are perfectly acceptable too). Add 1 tablespoon fresh lemon juice to orange or pineapple juice to balance the acidity.

In a nonreactive saucepan, reduce the juice over medium-high heat to a syrup, no more than ¼ cup. Add an equal amount of the appropriate oil:

CRANBERRY	Clear Orange Oil
ORANGE	Basil Oil
PINEAPPLE	Cilantro Oil
PINK GRAPEFRUIT	Tarragon Oil
POMEGRANATE	Ginger Oil

This will make a "broken" sauce, one that separates on the plate. For a somewhat more homogenized sauce, you can whisk very vigorously just before serving.

Store, tightly covered, in the refrigerator up to 2 weeks.

MAKES ABOUT ½ CUP

M I S C E L L A N E O U S O I L S

The remaining oils are easy, but not easily categorized. Each follows its own method, and several should be prepared a little in advance.

LOBSTER OIL	CARROT-CINNAMON OIL
SHRIMP OIL	BELL PEPPER OIL
PEANUT OIL	BEET-GINGER OIL
TRUFFLE OIL	CLEAR ORANGE OIL
CHIVE OIL	DILL OIL
TOMATO OIL	WATERCRESS OIL

■

L O B S T E R   O I L

2 pounds lobster shells, including the heads*
½ cup canola oil
1 medium carrot, peeled and diced
1 medium onion, peeled and diced
1 stalk celery, peeled and diced
1 clove garlic, peeled and chopped
1 bunch tarragon
1 bay leaf
1 bunch parsley, chopped
½ bottle dry white wine
4 cups canola oil

Crush the lobster shells (a heavy rolling pin is excellent for this).

In a large, high-sided pot, heat ½ cup canola oil until very hot. Carefully add the crushed lobster shells and stir well. Cook over high heat, stirring constantly, for 15 minutes.

Stir in the vegetables and herbs thoroughly. Add the wine. Continue cooking, stirring occasionally, for 15 minutes longer. Add the remaining 4 cups oil and reduce the heat to medium. Cook, stirring occasionally, for ½ hour.

Take the pot off the heat. When the mixture is no longer steaming, cover and let it sit at room temperature overnight. It is important to leave the mixture in the pot, as this will intensify the flavor. Do not refrigerate!

Strain the oil through a paper coffee filter into a clean container. Store, tightly covered, in the refrigerator up to 1 month.

MAKES 2½ TO 3 CUPS

*Lobster shells can be obtained at most fish markets. If you can get only cooked (bright red-orange) shells, that is fine, but try to get uncooked shells. If cooked shells are used, they should be cooked only 10 minutes in the oil.

SHRIMP OIL

Garnish the oil on a serving plate with some diced tomato and parsley for a very striking presentation.

> 1 pound shrimp shells*
> ½ cup canola oil
> 1 medium carrot, peeled and diced
> 1 medium onion, peeled and diced
> 1 stalk celery, peeled and diced
> 1 bunch thyme
> 1 bunch tarragon
> 1 bay leaf
> 1 bunch parsley, chopped
> ½ bottle dry white wine
> 6 cups canola oil

Crush the shrimp shells (a heavy rolling pin is excellent for this).

In a large, high-sided pot, heat ½ cup canola oil until very hot. Carefully add the shrimp shells and stir well. Cook over high heat, stirring constantly, for 15 minutes.

Stir in the vegetables and herbs thoroughly. Add the wine. Continue cooking, stirring oc-casionally, for 15 minutes longer. Add the remaining 6 cups oil and reduce the heat to medium. Cook, stirring occasionally, for ½ hour.

Take the pot off the heat. When the mixture is no longer steaming, cover and let it sit at room temperature overnight. It is important to leave the mixture in the pot, as this will intensify the flavor. Do not refrigerate!

Strain the oil through a paper coffee filter into a clean container. Store, tightly covered, in the refrigerator for up to 1 month.

MAKES ABOUT 4 CUPS

*Shrimp shells can be obtained at most fish markets. Try to find uncooked shells; if only cooked shells are available, cook them in oil only 10 minutes. The color of this oil will not be as bright orange as that of Lobster Oil, but the flavor is very pronounced and rich. Shrimp oil is an excellent substitution in reci-pes calling for Lobster Oil.

PEANUT OIL

1 pound raw skinless peanuts*
2 seventeen-ounce bottles canola oil

Roast the peanuts in a 250-degree oven until pale gold or amber in color. Let them cool slightly, then process to a paste in a food processor or blender. Combine the paste and oil. Shake well to combine, then strain through a paper coffee filter into a clean container. Store, tightly covered, at room temperature for up to 2 weeks. Do not refrigerate.

MAKES ABOUT 6 CUPS

*If raw peanuts are not available, use unsalted, roasted peanuts and omit roasting.

■

TRUFFLE OIL

2 medium truffles (fresh or canned)
¼ cup truffle juice (from canned truffles) or
*   port wine*
1 cup canola oil

Put the truffles and truffle juice in a blender. Blend to a smooth purée. Add the oil. Blend until smooth and emulsified. Do not strain. Store, tightly covered, in the refrigerator for up to 2 weeks.

MAKES 1½ CUPS

CHIVE OIL

The one difficulty with this recipe is obtaining enough chives. If you have less than 3 ounces, use what you have. Measure the juice and add 1½ times as much olive oil.

2 large bunches chives (3 ounces)
¾ cup extra virgin olive oil

Rinse the chives in water. Do not pat them dry; the excess water that clings to them will increase the juice.

Put the chives through a juice extractor. You should have ½ cup of juice.

Put the chive juice in a food processor or blender. Add the olive oil. Process until thoroughly blended. Store, tightly covered, in the refrigerator until slightly less liquid (about 1 hour). Chive Oil will keep as long as 4 days.

MAKES 1¼ CUPS

TOMATO OIL

4 large Beefsteak or plum tomatoes
¼ cup extra virgin olive oil
1 tablespoon chopped thyme*

Put the tomatoes, unpeeled, through a juice extractor. You should have 3 cups of juice. In a saucepan over medium-high heat, reduce the tomato juice by two-thirds to about 1 cup. Strain through a fine mesh strainer into a clean saucepan. Reduce to a syrup, no more than ½ cup. Stir in the olive oil and thyme. Store, tightly covered, in the refrigerator for up to 2 weeks.

MAKES ¾ CUP

*Instead of thyme, try minced fresh basil.

CARROT-CINNAMON OIL

2 tablespoons ground cinnamon
2 teaspoons water
1 cup canola oil
1 stick cinnamon
10 medium carrots, peeled
About 3 drops sherry vinegar

Mix ground cinnamon with water to a smooth paste. Put the paste in a clean jar. Add the oil and shake to blend well. Add the cinnamon stick. Let sit for about 2 days, until oil and cinnamon separate. Remove the oil on top with a ladle, being careful not to disturb the solids at the bottom too much. Discard the solids. Filter the oil—not the solids—through a paper coffee filter.

Put the carrots through a juice extractor. You should have 2 cups of juice. In a small saucepan over medium-high heat, reduce the carrot juice to 1 cup. Strain through a fine mesh strainer into a clean saucepan and reduce to a syrup, no more than ½ cup. Stir in ¼ cup cinnamon oil and mix well. Season with vinegar.

MAKES ABOUT ¾ CUP

BELL PEPPER OIL

The trick here is to reduce the juice slowly and, when it is a syrup, not to add too much olive oil. The resulting oil will be thick and very sweet. Use peppers all of one color, whether they be yellow, red or green. Let it come to room temperature before shaking and serving.

8 or 9 large bell peppers, cored and seeded
¼ cup extra virgin olive oil

Put the peppers through a juice extractor. You should have 2 cups of juice. In a saucepan over medium-high heat, slowly reduce the pepper juice by three-fourths, to about ½ cup. Strain through a fine mesh strainer into a clean saucepan. Reduce to a syrup, no more than ¼ cup. Stir in the olive oil thoroughly. Store, tightly covered, in the refrigerator up to 2 weeks.

MAKES ½ CUP

BEET-GINGER OIL

8 medium beets (about 2 pounds)
3 drops sherry vinegar
2 tablespoons Ginger Oil (page 45)

Put the beets through a juice extractor. You should have 2 cups of juice. In a saucepan over medium heat, reduce the beet juice to ½ cup. Strain through a fine mesh strainer into a clean saucepan and reduce to a syrup, no more than ¼ cup. Stir in the vinegar and Ginger Oil. Store, tightly covered, in the refrigerator up to 2 weeks.

MAKES ABOUT ⅓ CUP

■

CLEAR ORANGE OIL

Grated zest of 3 oranges
2 cups canola oil

Combine the zest and oil thoroughly. Let infuse for 2 days.

Strain the mixture through a paper coffee filter. Store, tightly covered, in the refrigerator up to 6 months.

MAKES 2 CUPS

DILL OIL

Dill gives off more juice in the spring and summer (this seems to be true of many herbs and vegetables), and the yield will vary from bunch to bunch. Simply add the same amount of olive oil as dill juice.

1 bunch dill
About ½ cup extra virgin olive oil

Put the dill through a juice extractor. Measure the dill juice and add an equal amount of oil.

Store, tightly covered, in the refrigerator up to 2 weeks.

MAKES ABOUT 1 CUP

WATERCRESS OIL

The proportion here, as in the case of Chive Oil, is 1½ times as much olive oil as juice. If you have less than ½ cup watercress juice, adjust the amount of oil to be added.

2 bunches watercress
¾ cup extra virgin olive oil

Put the watercress through a juice extractor. You should have ½ cup of juice.

Put the watercress juice in a food processor or blender. Add the olive oil and process until thoroughly blended. Store, tightly covered, in the refrigerator up to 2 weeks.

MAKES 1¼ CUPS

TUNA TARTARE WITH GAUFRETTE POTATOES

This is my version of the classic steak tartare with *pommes frites*. This tartare combines the soft texture of the ground tuna with the crispness of the gaufrette potatoes. If you don't have a mandoline, you can cut the potato chips by hand. If *really* pressed for time, use good-quality chips straight from the bag.

When buying the tuna, look for fish that is a deep shade of pink, almost red.

> ¾ *pound raw tuna, ground (mince by hand*
>   *or use a food processor)*
> ¼ *cup extra virgin olive oil*
> *3 tablespoons chopped chives*
> *A few drops tabasco*
> *Salt and freshly ground pepper to taste*
> *Gaufrette Potatoes (right)*
>
> *Garnish: 12 chives, cut into 3-inch lengths*
>   *Salmon roe or flying fish eggs*
>   *4 teaspoons Chive Oil (page 51)*

Combine all ingredients except Gaufrette Potatoes and Garnish and mix thoroughly. Cover tightly and refrigerate.

For each serving, make 3 little towers, layering tuna between 3 gaufrettes. Insert 1 chive stick through each tower.

Scatter the roe around each plate and drizzle with a little Chive Oil.

GAUFRETTE POTATOES

> *4 medium Idaho potatoes, peeled and*
>   *trimmed into large ovals*
> *Canola oil, for frying*

Using a mandoline set for "gaufrettes" (waffle pattern), slice the potatoes very thin. (If you do not have a mandoline, potatoes may be thinly sliced by hand). You will need 36 slices. Rinse potatoes in a bowl of cold water and pat dry with paper toweling.

Heat the oil (1-inch deep) until very hot (350 to 375 degrees). Fry the potato slices in batches (so they don't overlap) on both sides until golden brown and crisp, 5 to 8 minutes. (Potatoes may be baked in the oven instead of frying. They will be crisper and somewhat drier. After slicing potatoes, place on a nonstick baking sheet and brush with butter. Bake in a 450-degree oven until golden brown). Drain on paper toweling and salt them lightly. Set aside.

SERVES 4

TUNA TARTARE WITH ASSORTED CHIPS AND OILS

This version of tuna tartare makes little "sand-wiches" of the tuna between small vegetable chips. The brilliant colors of the oils are breath-taking. Drizzle the oils around the plate. You'll begin to believe you are an artist after you "paint" a plate or two.

Serve the dish without knives and forks and let your guests use their hands.

> 24 Vegetable Chips, any combination of
> Celeriac, Beet and Lotus Root (pages 196
> to 197)
> Tuna Tartare (page 55) without Gaufrettes
> or Garnish
> 2 teaspoons each red Bell Pepper Oil
> (page 46), Curry Oil (page 44) and Chive
> Oil (page 51)

Make 3 types of vegetable chips. This may be done up to 1 day in advance.

Prepare the Tuna Tartare. Shape the mixture into small balls no more than ¾ inch across.

For each serving, sandwich 3 tuna balls be-tween 2 vegetable chips.

Tuna Tartare with Oils; garnishes *clockwise from upper left*: fried eggplant skin, Gaufrette Potatoes, Beet Chip, fried basil, Lotus Root Chip.

Place 3 sandwiches on each of 4 serving plates. Drizzle a little of each oil around the plates.

SERVES 4

COD IN A
HORSERADISH CRUST

*6 tablespoons unseasoned breadcrumbs,
fresh or commercial*
2 teaspoons sweet butter
*2 tablespoons freshly grated or commer-
cially prepared white horseradish*
½ tablespoon chopped rosemary
1 tablespoon chopped tarragon
1 tablespoon chopped chervil
1 tablespoon chopped thyme
1 cup dry white wine
4 six-ounce cod fillets
Salt and freshly ground pepper to taste
½ cup Horseradish Oil (page 45)
¼ cup balsamic vinegar

Heat the oven to 450 degrees.

Combine the breadcrumbs, butter, horseradish, rosemary, tarragon, chervil and thyme
in the workbowl of a food processor. Add 3
tablespoons of the wine and process to a
paste.

Spread the top of each piece of cod with
equal amounts of the breadcrumbs mixture.

Place fillets in a shallow, broiler-proof pan.
Pour the remaining wine around them and
bake for 10 minutes.

Remove pan from the oven and place it
about 3 inches under a preheated broiler.
Season fillets with salt and pepper. Broil until
the crust is browned.

Place a fillet on each of 4 warmed serving
plates. Drizzle Horseradish Oil around the
cod and sprinkle a little balsamic vinegar
over all.

SERVES 4

COD CAKES WITH ORANGE-BASIL OIL

Cod and potatoes make wonderful little cakes. Add the chopped basil or not, as you like. The mixture should not be too moist. Cod cakes are also delicious with the simple Mustard Wine Sauce on page 193.

    4 cups water
    1 cup dry white wine
    1 bay leaf
    2 branches thyme
    2 cloves garlic, peeled
    1 pound cod fillets
    3 large potatoes (2½ to 3 pounds), peeled
        and quartered
    6 tablespoons extra virgin olive oil
    ⅔ cup milk
    2 to 3 tablespoons chopped fresh basil or
        2 teaspoons dried basil
    Flour
    ½ cup Orange-Basil Oil (page 48)

Heat the oven to 400 degrees.

Combine the water, wine, bay leaf, thyme and 1 clove of garlic in a large sauté pan. Bring to a simmer over medium-low heat. Add the fish and poach for 10 minutes.

Remove the fish and gently pat dry.

Cook the potatoes in boiling salted water until tender when pierced with a fork, 15 to 20 minutes. Drain the potatoes and dry them in the oven for 10 minutes. Mash them by hand, using a potato masher or a fork. Add the remaining clove of garlic, minced, 3 tablespoons olive oil and the milk. Mix until smooth. Combine the fish and the potato mixture and mix thoroughly. Stir in the basil. Shape the mixture into small cakes, about 2 inches in diameter. Cover and refrigerate for 1 hour.

Dust each cake lightly with flour. Heat the remaining 3 tablespoons olive oil and sauté the cakes until golden brown, 2 to 3 minutes per side. Serve with Orange-Basil Oil.

SERVES 4

Cod Cakes with Orange-Basil Oil

HALIBUT WITH TRUFFLE AND YELLOW BELL PEPPER OIL

The green of the fava beans, the yellow of the pepper oil and the black of the truffle oil make this a striking dish. While the flavor of Truffle Oil is unique, you can substitute red Bell Pepper Oil for an equally distinctive dish. If you like, substitute lima beans for the fava beans.

> *1 cup shelled fava beans*
> *3 tablespoons sweet butter*
> *4 seven-ounce halibut fillets*
> *Salt and freshly ground pepper to taste*
> *6 tablespoons Truffle Oil (page 51) or red*
> *   Bell Pepper Oil (page 53)*
> *6 tablespoons yellow Bell Pepper Oil*
> *   (page 53)*

Cook fava beans in boiling salted water until tender, about 5 minutes. Drain and pat dry. Set aside.

In a sauté pan, cook the halibut fillets in 2 tablespoons butter over medium heat until light brown on both sides, about 2 minutes per side. Remove from pan, season with salt and pepper and keep warm.

Add the beans and remaining tablespoon butter to the pan. Sauté over medium-high heat until hot. Season with salt and pepper. Place a fillet on each of 4 warmed serving plates. Spoon fava beans over the fish. Drizzle the two oils around the plate and serve.

SERVES 4

RED SNAPPER IN POTATO FLAKES WITH TOMATO OIL

It has been fashionable to prepare various foods in a potato crust. I think that while "strong" foods such as lamb can take a crunchy crust, fish and scallops are over-powered by such a coating. For a delicate potato crust, give fish a light coating of potato flakes. The idea is to keep moisture in the fish without overpowering its delicate flavor.

> *3 eggs*
> *4 seven-ounce red snapper fillets*
> *1 cup instant potato flakes*
> *½ cup extra virgin olive oil*
> *Salt and freshly ground pepper to taste*
> *½ cup Tomato Oil (page 52)*

Beat the eggs in a shallow bowl. Dip the red snapper fillets in the beaten egg, then dredge them lightly in potato flakes. Pat the flakes onto the fish so the fillets are nicely coated.

In a sauté pan, heat the olive oil over medium-high heat. Cook the fillets 1 minute per side. Season with salt and pepper.

Transfer the fillets to warmed serving plates. Drizzle with Tomato Oil.

SERVES 4

SEA SCALLOPS WITH GARLIC AND SAFFRON OIL

This dish boasts the classic combination of saffron and garlic that makes *bouillabaisse* so special. For a striking variation, make a purée of cooked beets and beat in a little butter. Fill the scallops with this mixture and refrigerate, tightly covered, overnight. The scallops will turn bright pink. Sauté them and serve with a vinaigrette of fresh lemon juice, good olive oil and some white, creamy-crumbly goat cheese mixed in.

10 cloves garlic, peeled
6 tablespoons extra virgin olive oil
1½ pounds large sea scallops
4 medium Idaho potatoes
2 tablespoons sherry vinegar
1 tablespoon chopped chives
2 tablespoons Clarified Butter (page 194) or extra virgin olive oil
½ cup Saffron Oil (page 44) or Tomato Oil (page 52)

Blanch the garlic in boiling water for 15 seconds; drain and repeat 3 times, changing the water each time. Purée in a small food processor or blender. Add 2 tablespoons olive oil and blend again until smooth.

Cut a small pocket into the side of each scallop and pipe in about ½ teaspoon of the garlic purée. Cover tightly and refrigerate until needed.

Peel the potatoes. Cook them whole in boiling salted water until tender when pierced with a fork, 15 to 20 minutes.

Drain and cut into ½-inch slices. Mix with the vinegar, chives and remaining 4 tablespoons olive oil.

If scallops are wet, lightly pat dry. Melt the butter over medium-high heat and sauté the scallops until golden brown on both sides. Serve with the potato salad and a drizzle of Saffron Oil.

S E R V E S   4

SHRIMP SALAD WITH CURRY OIL

This is another warm-and-cold salad, made that much more special by the addition of vanilla grains to the Curry Oil.

> 6 whole Jerusalem artichokes or 6 globe
> artichoke bases, quartered
> 2 tablespoons fresh lemon juice
> 2- to 3-inch piece vanilla bean
> ½ cup Curry Oil (page 44)
> 2 tablespoons extra virgin olive oil
> 1 small bunch cilantro, chopped
> Salt, freshly ground pepper and paprika to
> taste
> 24 large shrimp, peeled and deveined
> 2 tablespoons sweet butter
> 2 cups mixed salad greens

Peel the Jerusalem artichokes and slice very thin. Place them in a bowl of cold water and 1 tablespoon lemon juice until ready to cook.

Split the vanilla bean in half lengthwise and scrape the soft grains into a small bowl (re-serve the bean for another use). Add the Curry Oil to the vanilla grains and mix well. Set aside.

Whisk together the olive oil, the remaining 1 tablespoon lemon juice and the chopped cilantro. Season with salt and pepper and set aside.

Steam the shrimp as directed on page 104 until they are pink throughout, 3 to 4 minutes. Season with salt and paprika.

Drain the artichoke slices. In a medium sauté pan, melt the butter and sauté the artichokes until tender. Season with salt and pepper.

Arrange the salad greens in the center of a large plate. Place the sautéed artichokes around the greens. Toss the cooked shrimp in the cilantro vinaigrette and arrange them on the greens. Spoon vinaigrette over the shrimp and drizzle a little Curry Oil over all.

SERVES 4

Shrimp Salad with Curry Oil

SHRIMP SKEWERS WITH OYSTERS AND HORSERADISH OIL

Usually, a seafood mousse is baked. Here, shrimp mousse becomes a crisp-fried coating for large, succulent shrimp.

> 12 medium shrimp, peeled and deveined
> 1 egg white
> 1 cup heavy cream
> Salt and cayenne pepper to taste
> 24 large shrimp, peeled and deveined
> 1 cup unseasoned breadcrumbs, fresh or commercial
> 1 cup extra virgin olive oil
> 8 oysters, with their liquor
> ½ cup Horseradish Oil (page 45)

Combine the medium shrimp, egg white, cream, and salt and cayenne pepper in a food processor or blender. Process until smooth. Refrigerate mousse until ready to use.

Thread 3 large shrimp on each of 8 skewers. Using a pastry bag, pipe mousse over the shrimp to cover. Dip the shrimp in breadcrumbs to coat. Set aside in the refrigerator on plastic wrap for 30 minutes or until ready to use.

In a large sauté pan or Chinese wok, heat about ½ inch olive oil to 375 degrees. Fry the shrimp until golden brown on all sides, about 5 minutes.

Chop the oysters coarsely and mix them and their liquor with the Horseradish Oil.

Serve 2 skewers per person with the oyster-horseradish sauce.

SERVES 4

COLD CUCUMBER SOUP WITH DILL OIL

A variation on the first cold soup I made in Thailand when sent there by Louis Outhier. The hot shrimp are exquisite against the backdrop of ice-cold cucumber soup and the pungency of Dill Oil. A wonderful summer dish.

> 2 cucumbers, peeled, seeded and coarsely chopped
> 1 cup plain yogurt
> 1 tablespoon chopped dill
> Salt and cayenne pepper to taste
> 6 tablespoons sour cream
> 12 large shrimp, peeled and deveined
> ¼ cup Dill Oil (page 54)
>
> Garnish: 4 sprigs dill

Combine the cucumbers, yogurt, 1 tablespoon dill, and salt and cayenne pepper in a food processor or blender. Process until smooth.

Combine the cucumber mixture with the sour cream in a medium bowl. Set the bowl in a larger bowl that has been filled with ice and stir occasionally until cool, or cover tightly and refrigerate until cold. Don't prepare the shrimp until the soup is cold.

Steam the shrimp for 1 minute until they are pink. Lightly season with salt and cayenne pepper. Pour the soup into chilled bowls and add the hot shrimp. Garnish with dill sprigs and Dill Oil.

SERVES 4

SOFT SHELL CRABS WITH CARROT-CINNAMON OIL

This is one of the rare cases where it's best to season the food before cooking. The crab shells protect the meat from the drying effect of salt.

> 8 medium soft shell crabs, dressed
> Salt and cayenne pepper to taste
> 3 tablespoons sweet butter
> 1 teaspoon chopped chervil
> 1 teaspoon chopped cilantro
> 1 teaspoon chopped dill
> 1 teaspoon chopped sorrel
> 1 teaspoon chopped parsley
> 1 teaspoon chopped tarragon
> 1 teaspoon chopped chives
> 1 teaspoon chopped thyme
> 1 teaspoon chopped marjoram
> ½ cup Carrot-Cinnamon Oil (page 52)

Season crabs with salt and pepper. In a large sauté pan, melt the butter over medium-high heat. Add the crabs and sauté 2 minutes per side. Scatter the herbs over the crabs and cook for 2 minutes longer. Serve 2 crabs per person with a drizzle of Carrot-Cinnamon Oil.

SERVES 4

TERRINE OF PASTA AND CRABMEAT

The trick to this dish (I think of it as one of my "signature dishes") is to line the mold with plastic wrap so the unmolding is foolproof. This trick works beautifully for any terrine that requires unmolding.

You can make the broth and stuff the ziti the day before, or even assemble the terrine the night before. The dish may sound complicated, but it really isn't. Take your time and you'll be amazed at the extraordinary result.

> 1 pound ziti
> ½ pound crabmeat, picked over for cartilage
> 1 bunch cilantro
> Salt and freshly ground pepper to taste
> 2 cups Lobster Broth (right)
> 1 stalk lemon grass
> 2 tablespoons fresh lime juice
> 1 teaspoon harissa pepper or Chinese chili paste
> 1 tablespoon unflavored gelatin
> ½ cup Lobster Oil (page 49) or Shrimp Oil (page 50)

Cook the ziti in boiling salted water until *al dente* (firm, not mushy). Drain immediately and rinse under cold running water. Set aside.

Combine the crabmeat and cilantro in a food processor or blender. Process until finely chopped. Season with salt and pepper.

Fit a pastry bag with a tip that can be inserted into the ziti. Pipe the crabmeat mixture to fill each piece of pasta.

Line a 1½-quart terrine mold with plastic wrap. Fill the mold with the stuffed ziti, layering them lengthwise in the same direction.

Heat the Lobster Broth, lemon grass, lime juice, harissa pepper, salt and pepper until hot. Sprinkle the gelatin over the broth and stir to dissolve. When the broth has cooled to room temperature, strain it over the stuffed ziti. Cover tightly and refrigerate overnight.

Unmold and slice about ½ inch thick. Serve with a drizzle of Lobster Oil. Garnish with cilantro leaves, if you like.

SERVES 15

LOBSTER BROTH

Follow the recipe for Lobster Oil (page 49) but add 1 bunch thyme with the herbs and decrease oil to ½ cup. When the wine has nearly evaporated, add 4 cups water (preferably bottled) and cook over medium-high heat for 20 minutes. Strain.

MAKES ABOUT 2 CUPS BROTH

Terrine of Pasta and Crabmeat

''SPIKED'' SWEETBREADS WITH RED BELL PEPPER OIL

Here we do something unusual—we sauté and roast the sweetbreads without blanching them first. Sweetbreads should never be served pink and blanching is the usual way to avoid that. Here, braising them in a flavorful liquid accomplishes the same thing.

7 tablespoons extra virgin olive oil
1 medium red bell pepper, seeded, deribbed
*   and cut into ¼-inch-wide strips*
4 six-ounce sweetbreads
3 tablespoons sweet butter
1 clove garlic, peeled and chopped
½ medium onion, peeled and chopped
¼ medium carrot, peeled and chopped
1 cup water
1 branch of thyme
4 bunches broccoli rabe
½ cup red Bell Pepper Oil (page 53)
Salt and freshly ground pepper to taste

Heat the oven to 550 degrees.

Heat 2 tablespoons olive oil over medium-high heat. Add the red pepper with a pinch of salt and sauté for 1 minute. "Spike" each sweetbread with 4 or 5 red pepper strips, threading them in one side of the sweetbread, through the center and out the other side.

Heat 3 tablespoons olive oil and the butter over medium-high heat. Add the sweetbreads and sauté until brown on both sides, about 5 minutes. Remove the sweetbreads to an ovenproof dish and scatter with the garlic, onion and carrot. Put in the oven and roast for 10 minutes. Add water and thyme and cook for 10 minutes longer.

Cook the broccoli rabe in boiling salted water for 5 minutes. Drain thoroughly and sauté in the remaining olive oil until hot.

Drain the sweetbreads, season with salt and pepper and slice ½ inch thick. Serve with broccoli rabe and a drizzle of red Bell Pepper Oil.

SERVES 4

RABBIT SAUSAGE WITH MUSTARD OIL

This incredibly easy preparation makes "sausage" without a machine to stuff forcemeat into casings. Rabbit liver gives the sausage a very distinctive flavor. It should be available from the butcher when you buy the rabbit. You may substitute duck, chicken or venison for the rabbit; use 1½ pounds of boneless meat.

Crimp the foil tightly so water doesn't get in.

> 1 three-pound rabbit, boned and cut into
>   ¼-inch dice
> 1 whole chicken breast, skinned, boned and
>   cut into ¼-inch dice
> 3½ ounces boiled ham, cut into ¼-inch dice
> 1 egg
> 3 ounces foie gras or rabbit or chicken liver,
>   cut into ¼-inch dice
> ¼ cup shelled pistachios, broken into halves,
>   or coarsely chopped, skinned hazelnuts
> Salt and freshly ground pepper to taste
> ½ cup Mustard Oil (page 44)

Mix all ingredients except Mustard Oil. Roll in aluminum foil in a long cylinder, about 1½ inches in diameter. Poach in simmering water for 12 minutes. Remove from heat and allow to cool in the water. Slice and serve with a drizzle of Mustard Oil.

SERVES 6

MARINATED LEMON CHICKEN WITH FENNEL OIL

> 4 whole chicken breasts, halved, skinned and
>   boned
> 2 cups fresh lemon juice
> 2 tablespoons chopped cilantro
> 1 tablespoon chopped parsley
> 1 tablespoon chopped chives
> 1 tablespoon chopped basil
> 1 tablespoon chopped tarragon
> 1 tablespoon chopped chervil
> 2 tablespoons sweet butter
> ¼ cup extra virgin olive oil
> Salt and freshly ground pepper to taste
> ½ cup Fennel Oil (page 44)

In a deep bowl, combine the chicken, lemon juice and herbs. Marinate for 10 minutes. Drain chicken, reserving marinade.

In large sauté pan, melt the butter over medium-high heat. Add the chicken and sauté 4 minutes per side. Remove from the pan and season with salt and pepper. Deglaze the pan with ¼ cup of the marinade. Whisk in the olive oil and bring to a boil. Pour sauce over the chicken. Serve with a drizzle of Fennel Oil.

SERVES 4

GRILLED VEAL WITH LOBSTER BEARNAISE

This dish is a double tribute to the great cuisinier Escoffier. It brings together Escoffier's concept of mixing meat and shellfish with the master's Béarnaise sauce.

1½-pound lobster
4 slices veal (about 5 ounces each), pounded thin
1 tablespoon sweet butter
Salt and freshly ground pepper to taste
2 egg yolks
½ cup water
1 cup Lobster Oil (page 49) or Shrimp Oil (page 50)
1 tablespoon chopped tarragon
3 drops fresh lemon juice

Cook lobster in boiling salted water for 2 minutes. Drain and let cool. Remove the meat from the tail and claws. Dice and set aside.

Grill the veal (or sauté in 1 tablespoon sweet butter) until desired doneness. Season with salt and pepper and keep warm.

In a double boiler, whisk together egg yolks and water with a pinch of salt. Cook over boiling water, whisking constantly, until light, fluffy and slightly thickened. Add the oil in a very thin stream, whisking constantly. Fold in the lobster and tarragon. Add lemon juice and season with salt and pepper. Serve with the veal.

SERVES 4

SAUTEED CALVES' LIVER WITH BEET-GINGER OIL

2 tablespoons sweet butter
4 seven-ounce slices calves' liver
Salt and freshly ground pepper to taste
Potato Purée (below)
Braised Red Cabbage (page 71)

Garnish: Beet Chips (page 196)
½ cup Beet-Ginger Oil (page 53)

Melt the butter over medium-high heat and sauté the liver 1 minute per side. Season with salt and pepper. Serve with Potato Purée and Braised Red Cabbage, and garnish with Beet Chips and Beet-Ginger Oil.

SERVES 4

POTATO PUREE

4 medium purple or Idaho potatoes, peeled and halved
¾ cup milk, warmed
1 tablespoon sweet butter
Salt

Cook potatoes in boiling salted water until tender when pierced with a fork, 15 to 20 minutes. Beat in the warm milk and butter. Season with salt.

BRAISED RED CABBAGE

2 tablespoons sweet butter
½ medium onion, thinly sliced
1 pound red cabbage, shredded
Zest of 1 medium orange
½ cup red wine vinegar
½ cup red wine
3 tablespoons blueberries
Salt and freshly ground pepper to taste

In a nonreactive pot, melt the butter over medium-high heat; add the onion and cook until translucent. Add the cabbage, orange zest, vinegar and wine. Cover and cook for 15 minutes. Add the blueberries and cook until cabbage is tender, about 15 minutes longer. Season with salt and pepper.

VENISON WITH CRANBERRY-ORANGE OIL

1½ cups dry red wine
3 tablespoons extra virgin olive oil
2 tablespoons crushed, unsweetened cranberries
4 seven-ounce venison fillets
2 tablespoons sweet butter
1 cup Onion Jam (page 163)
½ cup Cranberry-Orange Oil (page 48)

Combine the wine, 1 tablespoon olive oil and the cranberries. Marinate the venison in this mixture for 1 day.

Heat the oven to 450 degrees. In a large sauté pan, melt the butter and 2 tablespoons olive oil over medium-high heat until golden brown. Remove the venison from the marinade; do not pat dry. Sauté 1½ minutes per side, until golden brown. Remove to an ovenproof pan and roast 10 minutes for medium-rare.

Meanwhile, deglaze the sauté pan with the marinade. Reduce to a syrup, no more than ¼ cup. When the venison is cooked to taste, coat each fillet with the reduced syrup and keep warm.

Put a scant ¼ cup Onion Jam on each of 4 warmed serving plates. Cut each fillet into 3 slices and arrange over the Onion Jam. Drizzle with Cranberry-Orange Oil.

SERVES 4

BUILDING BLOCK: VEGETABLE BROTHS

An important part of my cuisine is the use of vegetable broths. Unlike the beef, veal, chicken, fish and shellfish stocks of classic French cuisine, which routinely take as long as 10 hours to prepare, vegetable broths are cooked in 30 minutes.

The broths can be served alone or in combination with flavored and unflavored oils to make uniquely aromatic sauces, perfect accompaniments to fast sautés and steamed dishes; use about ½ cup per serving. Some of my recipes call for the basic broths that follow just as they are, and some work their own variation on the broth theme.

All of the vegetable broths will keep, tightly covered, in the refrigerator for 3 to 4 days. Better yet, freeze them for as long as 1 month.

BASIC VEGETABLE BROTHS

SHALLOT BROTH · MUSHROOM BROTH · MIXED VEGETABLE BROTH · ENDIVE BROTH · ARTICHOKE BROTH

Each of these broths has a unique, rich flavor, amazing considering the short cooking time. I have always been fascinated with the Mushroom Broth and its reduction which, after a mere 30 minutes, closely resembles a veal stock and, if reduced further, a veal *demi-glace* that would take a day to prepare.

Shallot Broth with Flounder (page 76) garnished with fried shallot rings, Squab and Lentil Salad (page 35)

SHALLOT BROTH

1 tablespoon extra virgin olive oil
1 tablespoon sweet butter
¾ pound shallots, peeled and thinly sliced
  (3 cups)
2 cups water (just enough to cover shallots)
Salt and freshly ground pepper to taste

In a pan large enough to hold the shallots in a shallow layer, heat the olive oil and butter over medium-high heat until sizzling. Add the shallots with a pinch of salt and pepper. Sauté over medium-high heat for 10 to 15 minutes, until the shallots are very brown and have caramelized.

Add just enough water to cover the shallots. Stir well, scraping up any browned bits clinging to the pan. Transfer the shallots and broth to a smaller pot.

The water should just cover the shallots; add a little more if necessary.

Boil over medium-high heat for 15 minutes. Strain broth through a fine mesh strainer.

MUSHROOM BROTH

2 tablespoons sweet butter
1 pound white button mushrooms, quartered
  (about 5 cups)
Salt and freshly ground pepper to taste
2 shallots, peeled and sliced
1 clove garlic, peeled and halved
2 cups water (just enough to cover
  mushrooms)
2 tablespoons minced parsley

In a pan large enough to hold the mushrooms in a single layer, heat the butter over medium-high heat until sizzling. Add the mushrooms with a pinch of salt and pepper and cook, stirring constantly, until the mushrooms are deep brown and have caramelized, 15 to 20 minutes.

Add the shallots, garlic and just enough water to cover the mushrooms. Add the parsley and stir well, scraping up any browned bits clinging to the pan. Transfer the vegetables and broth to a smaller pot.

Bring to a boil over medium-high heat and boil for 15 minutes. Strain broth through a fine mesh strainer. The broth will be deep brown in color.

MUSHROOM SYRUP

Mushroom Broth may be reduced over medium-high heat for about 10 minutes longer until just a syrup remains, no more than ½ cup. This syrup resembles a veal *demi-glace*. Serve alone as an intensely flavored sauce.

For a sauce with milder flavor, swirl in 2 to 3 tablespoons olive oil or sauce individual servings with 1 tablespoon each Mushroom Syrup and olive oil. Even when the oil is whisked in, the effect on serving will be of a "broken sauce," the gold of the oil and rich brown of the Mushroom Syrup separating slightly—a look I love.

■

MIXED VEGETABLE BROTH

Mixed Vegetable Broth perfectly complements a sauté of chicken, fish or shellfish.

4 cups mixed vegetables, coarsely chopped*
1 bunch parsley
½ cup fresh herbs (any kind)
2 tablespoons extra virgin olive oil (optional)

Put the vegetables, parsley and other herbs in a medium-size pot and cover with water.

Boil over medium-high heat for 20 minutes. Strain the broth through a fine mesh strainer. Serve alone or swirl in 2 tablespoons olive oil.

*Carrots, zucchini, celery, onions, turnips, mushrooms, cabbage and garlic.

ENDIVE BROTH

3 medium heads endive, thinly sliced (3 cups)
2 tablespoons sweet butter
Salt and freshly ground pepper to taste
2 cups dry white wine (just enough to cover endives)
2 tablespoons peanut oil (optional)

In a pan large enough to hold endives in a shallow layer, sauté the endives in 2 tablespoons butter with a large pinch of salt and pepper over medium-high heat for 5 minutes. Endives will be soft.

Add just enough wine to cover the endives. Bring to a boil, then reduce the heat to medium-low. Simmer, uncovered, for 15 minutes.

Strain broth through a fine mesh strainer. Serve alone or add 2 tablespoons peanut oil to round out the flavor and make the sauce less acidic.

ARTICHOKE BROTH

4 large or 6 medium artichokes*
Fresh lemon juice
2 tablespoons extra virgin olive oil
½ small onion, peeled and chopped
3 to 4 cups dry white wine (just enough to
   cover artichokes)
1 teaspoon salt

Trim the hard base from each artichoke. Trim the top down to the fuzzy choke.

Remove all the leaves, trimming until you reach the heart, the rounded base of the artichoke.

Scrape away the choke. Put each trimmed artichoke in water acidulated with a little lemon juice and a pinch of salt (this will prevent discoloration).

In a medium saucepan, heat the olive oil over medium heat. Add the onion and let it sweat in the olive oil for 5 minutes.

Cut each artichoke heart into quarters and add them to the onions.

Add just enough wine to cover the artichokes and the salt. Boil over medium-high heat for 20 minutes. Strain broth through a fine mesh strainer.

*If you are pressed for time, the frozen artichoke hearts available in most supermarkets can be used. Simply thaw, quarter and proceed with the recipe.

SHALLOT BROTH WITH FLOUNDER

Here is an unstrained variation of the intensely flavored basic Shallot Broth on page 74. While the basic broth is meant to be enjoyed as a sauce, this is a true broth, nearly a soup.

4 tablespoons sweet butter
½ pound shallots, peeled and sliced (2 cups)
2 cups water
4 seven-ounce flounder fillets
2 tablespoons hazelnut or extra virgin olive
   oil
1 teaspoon chopped marjoram plus 4 sprigs
   marjoram, for garnish
Salt and freshly ground pepper to taste

In a large sauté pan, melt the butter over low heat. Add the shallots and a pinch of salt and cook until shallots have caramelized. Add water and simmer for 20 minutes.

Add the fish fillets and poach them for 3 minutes. Gently remove to soup plates. Stir in the hazelnut oil and marjoram; season the broth with salt and pepper. Ladle broth over each serving of fish and garnish with a sprig of marjoram.

SERVES 4

WATERCRESS BROTH WITH YELLOW PIKE

This dish combines two water-loving ingredients: yellow pike and watercress. The intense, peppery flavor of watercress is a delicious foil for the delicate yellow pike. Add the watercress to the fish broth only at the last moment, to preserve its sharp flavor and bright color.

> 2 tablespoons sweet butter
> 1 medium onion, peeled and thinly sliced
> 1 leek, washed thoroughly and thinly sliced
> 1 stalk celery, chopped
> 1 three-pound yellow pike or salmon, filleted, head and bones reserved
> 2 cups dry white wine
> 4 cups water
> ½ cup sliced button mushrooms
> 1 bunch watercress, leaves and stems separated
> 1 Bouquet Garni (page 194)
> Salt and freshly ground pepper to taste

In a large saucepan, melt the butter over medium-high heat; add the onion, leek, celery, fish bones and head. Gently cook until vegetables are soft and translucent. (Do not allow them to color.) Add the wine, water, mushrooms, watercress stems and Bouquet Garni. Simmer for 30 minutes. Strain the broth through a fine mesh strainer into a clean saucepan and keep warm over low heat.

Finely chop the watercress leaves. Cut the fish fillets into 3 × ½-inch strips. Heat the broth to a simmer and add the strips of fish. Poach the fish for 1 minute. Gently remove to soup plates. Season the broth with salt and pepper; stir in the chopped watercress. Ladle broth over each serving of fish.

SERVES 4

WHITING WITH ENDIVE BROTH

You will be amazed at how beautifully the tangy flavor of endive broth complements mellow whiting, a very delicate, white fish. In the place of my Peanut Oil you can use any commercial peanut oil, so long as it is from a first pressing. To crack peanuts, simply whack them with a heavy pot.

4 heads endive, 12 leaves reserved and
    remaining leaves chopped
3 tablespoons sweet butter
Pinch sugar
Salt and freshly ground pepper to taste
1 cup dry white wine
2 pounds whiting, cut into 12 pieces
1 tablespoon Peanut Oil (page 51) or roasted
    peanut oil
1 tablespoon cracked black pepper
2 tablespoons cracked raw peanuts

In a pan large enough to hold endives in a shallow layer, sauté the chopped endives over medium heat in 1 tablespoon butter with the sugar, salt and pepper for 5 minutes. Add the wine and cook until tender, about 15 minutes. Strain the broth through a fine mesh strainer, reserving the cooked endives; set the broth aside.

Combine the cooked endives with about 2 tablespoons broth in a food processor or blender and process until smooth. Set aside.

In a large sauté pan over medium heat, melt 1 tablespoon butter. Add the fillets to the pan. Cook 3 minutes per side. Remove them from the pan, season with salt and pepper and keep warm.

Sauté the 12 endive leaves in the remaining 1 tablespoon butter until they take on a little color around the edges, about 6 minutes. Heat the endive purée and the remaining broth in separate pans. Whisk the peanut oil into the broth.

Scatter the cracked pepper and peanuts around each of 4 serving plates. Spoon endive purée onto the center of each plate and top with 3 pieces of fish. Place one endive leaf on top of each piece of fish. Spoon some broth around the fish.

SERVES 4

Whiting with Endive Broth. Here, each piece of fish has been wrapped in endive leaves with a little of the endive purée. Chives tie the bundles.

MONKFISH WITH MUSHROOM SYRUP

Monkfish has been called "poor man's lobster." To me, it has the flavor and texture of meat. Monkfish fillets are thick and wide. Cut them in half lengthwise, then cut across. The flesh is soft enough that, when wrapped in bacon, pieces take on the shape of medallions.

This dish always reminds me of a real "meat and gravy" dish. To complete the presentation, serve this with a potato purée or Pommes Annette (page 150).

1 pound monkfish fillets
12 slices bacon, double-smoked if possible
¼ cup extra virgin olive oil
1 cup shiitake mushrooms, stems discarded and caps washed thoroughly
2 tablespoons chopped parsley
Salt and freshly ground pepper to taste
½ cup Mushroom Syrup (page 74)

Cut the monkfish fillets into 12 pieces. Encircle each piece with a slice of bacon and secure these fish medallions with a piece of kitchen string. In a large sauté pan, heat 1 tablespoon olive oil over medium-high heat until hot. Cook the medallions until golden brown on both sides, 5 minutes per side.

In a sauté pan, heat 1 tablespoon olive oil over medium-high heat until hot. Add the mushroom caps and sauté until soft and browned. Sprinkle with parsley and season with salt and pepper.

Warm the Mushroom Syrup and whisk in the remaining 2 tablespoons olive oil. Season with salt and pepper.

Arrange 3 medallions of each on 4 serving plates. Divide the sautéed mushrooms among the plates and spoon sauce around the fish.

SERVES 4

SALMON IN A SHIITAKE SHELL

Remember to look for large shiitake mushrooms. The salmon and shiitakes have the same texture; the contrast here is in the flavor.

8 large shiitake mushrooms, stems discarded and caps washed thoroughly

1½ pound salmon fillets (½ to ¾ inch thick), cut into 4 six-ounce pieces, trimmed into round shapes

½ cup all-purpose flour

2 cups unseasoned breadcrumbs, fresh or commercial

2 eggs

2 tablespoons sweet butter

½ cup Mushroom Syrup (page 74)

2 tablespoons hazelnut or extra virgin olive oil

2 tablespoons chopped parsley

Steam the mushroom caps over boiling water until soft, 4 to 5 minutes.

Sandwich each piece of salmon between two mushroom caps. Put the flour, breadcrumbs and the eggs, slightly beaten, in 3 separate bowls. Dip each salmon-mushroom piece first into the egg, then the flour and finally the breadcrumbs. Repeat the 3 coatings.

Melt the butter in a medium nonstick pan over medium-high heat. When hot, add the salmon-mushroom pieces and cook for 3 minutes per side for medium-rare. Remove from the pan and cover.

Warm the Mushroom Syrup and whisk in the hazelnut oil.

Place 1 salmon-mushroom piece on each of 4 warmed serving plates. Spoon some sauce around the plate and sprinkle with parsley.

SERVES 4

Following Pages: Monkfish with Mushroom Syrup, Salmon in a Shiitake Shell

LOBSTER A LA NAGE

This is one of the simplest and best methods of preparing lobster. Using a relatively small amount of cooking liquid and cooking the lobster in the shell bring out the strongest flavor and a natural sweetness.

> 4 one-and-a-half-pound lobsters
> ¾ cup sweet butter
> 1 medium carrot, peeled and julienned
> 1 medium turnip, peeled and julienned
> ½ stalk celery
> 1 medium leek, washed thoroughly and
>   julienned
> 2 shallots, peeled and finely chopped
> Salt and freshly ground pepper to taste
> 2 cups brut Champagne or dry sparkling
>   white wine
> 2 cups Mixed Vegetable Broth (page 75)
> 2 tablespoons chopped chervil

Heat the oven to 450 degrees.

Blanch the lobsters in boiling salted water for 2 minutes. Drain and set aside.

Melt 4 tablespoons butter in a pan. Add the vegetables (except 1 of the shallots), cover and sweat until tender but not soft. Season with salt and pepper. Set aside.

Cut the lobsters in half lengthwise. Separate the claws from the bodies and crack the shells. In a large pot, melt 2 tablespoons butter. Add the remaining shallot, lobsters, vegetables, Champagne and Mixed Vegetable Broth. Cover the pot and cook in the oven for 6 minutes.

Remove the lobster bodies from the pot and continue to cook the claws for 2 minutes longer. Remove claws from the pot.

Place the pot on the stove over high heat and reduce the liquid by half. Whisk in the remaining 6 tablespoons butter. Add the chervil. Serve the lobster, still in the shell if you like, in bowls with some of the broth and vegetables.

SERVES 4

LOBSTER WITH PARSNIP PUREE

The essence of any lobster preparation is sweetness and texture. This dish compares the distinctive sweetness and texture of the parsnips, lotus root and lobster.

> 4 one-and-a-half-pound lobsters
> 6 medium parsnips, peeled and diced
> 4 tablespoons sweet butter
> ½ cup heavy cream
> Salt and freshly ground pepper to taste
> ½ cup Mushroom Syrup (page 74)
> ¼ cup Lobster Oil (page 49) or Shrimp Oil (page 50)
>
> *Garnish: Lotus Root Chips (page 196–197)*

Blanch the lobsters in boiling salted water for 2 minutes. Let cool and remove meat from tails and claws.

Cook the parsnips in boiling salted water until tender. Drain and pass through a food mill or ricer. Add 2 tablespoons butter, the cream, and salt and pepper to taste, and keep warm.

Melt the remaining 2 tablespoons butter in a sauté pan over medium heat. Add the lobster meat and sauté on both sides, 3 minutes per side.

While the lobster is cooking, heat the Mushroom Syrup and whisk in the Lobster Oil.

Arrange the lobster on each of 4 warmed serving plates. Add some of the parsnip purée to each plate and garnish with Lotus Root Chips. Spoon some sauce around the lobster.

SERVES 4

■

SHRIMP IN A SPICED ORANGE AND SAUTERNES BROTH

This is a wonderful dish for a summer party. Let the guests help themselves from large serving bowls of shrimp and rice.

> 1 medium carrot, peeled and diced
> ¼ medium cucumber, peeled, seeded and diced
> 4 medium button mushrooms, diced
> 1 cup Sauternes or Gewürztraminer
> 1 cup fresh orange juice
> 2 tablespoons sweet butter
> 1 tablespoon fresh ginger julienne
> 8 threads saffron
> 1 tablespoon fresh lemon juice
> 32 large shrimp (about 2 pounds), peeled and deveined
> 2 tablespoons chopped flat-leaf parsley
> Salt and freshly ground pepper to taste
> 2 cups Spiced Rice (page 162)

In a large pot, combine the vegetables, Sauternes, orange juice, butter, ginger, saffron and lemon juice. Cook for 15 minutes. Add shrimp and cook for 1 minute. Add the parsley and salt and pepper to taste. Serve in bowls over Spiced Rice.

SERVES 4

CANNELLONI OF CRAB WITH CARDAMOM

6 tablespoons sweet butter
1 bunch Swiss chard, finely chopped
½ pound crabmeat, picked over for cartilage
¼ cup chopped parsley
Salt and freshly ground pepper to taste
4 spring roll or egg roll wrappers*
2 cups Mixed Vegetable Broth (page 75)
½ teaspoon cracked green cardamom seed*

Melt 2 tablespoons butter over medium-high heat and add the Swiss chard. Cook until tender, about 4 minutes. In a medium bowl, combine the Swiss chard with the crabmeat and parsley. Season with salt and pepper.

Cook the spring roll wrappers in boiling salted water until soft, about 15 seconds. Drain on paper toweling. Place 1½ to 2 tablespoons of the crabmeat mixture one each wrapper. Roll the wrappers around the filling into cylinder shapes. Steam over boiling water until heated through, about 5 minutes.

In a small saucepan, boil the Mixed Vegetable Broth with the cracked cardamom seeds until reduced by three-fourths. Whisk in the remaining 4 tablespoons butter and season with salt and pepper. Divide the cannelloni among 4 warmed serving plates and spoon some of the sauce over them.

SERVES 4

*For an even lighter variation, use rice paper instead of spring roll skins. Soften each 8-inch round of rice paper between layers of damp kitchen toweling for about 5 minutes, until pliable enough to roll without cracking, but not wet. The rounds of rice paper are much larger than spring roll wrappers. Fill them with twice as much crabmeat mixture; roll, then cut in half. Spring roll and egg roll wrappers and rice paper can be found in Oriental markets. Cardamom is a *very* potent spice, so be sure not to overpower the dish. Use green cardamom only, as it is less powerful than the white variety.

SCALLOPS WITH ARTICHOKE BROTH

½ cup shelled fava beans

4 medium artichokes

4 tablespoons extra virgin olive oil

Salt and freshly ground pepper to taste

2 tablespoons grated hard goat cheese or Parmesan

1 cup Artichoke Broth (page 76)

2 teaspoons chopped savory

2 tablespoons sweet butter

18 ounces scallops

Cook the fava beans in boiling salted water until tender, about 5 minutes. Drain and keep warm.

Trim the hard base from each artichoke. Trim the top down to the fuzzy choke. Remove all the leaves, trimming until you reach the heart, the rounded base of the artichoke. Scrape away the choke. (If you prepare the artichoke hearts in advance, save the trimmings to make Artichoke Broth. Put the trimmed artichokes in water acidulated with a little lemon juice and a pinch of salt to prevent them from discoloring.) Cut the artichokes into fine julienne strips. Heat 2 tablespoons olive oil over medium heat. Add the artichokes and season with salt and pepper. Sauté until hot, about 2 minutes. Remove them to a bowl and stir in the cheese. Set aside.

Reduce the Artichoke Broth by half and whisk in the remaining 2 tablespoons olive oil. Add the savory and the fava beans.

Melt the butter in a medium sauté pan over medium-high heat. Add the scallops and sauté until lightly brown on both sides. Season with salt and pepper. Divide among 4 warmed serving plates. Spoon sauce around the scallops and scatter reserved sautéed artichokes and cheese over all.

SERVES 4

LAMB IN A POTATO CRUST

This is one of the favorite dishes at Lafayette. The potato crust does not overpower the strong flavor and texture of the lamb. Be sure to sear the lamb quickly before covering it with the unwashed potato shreds. This searing seals in the juices. A nonstick pan is important for this recipe.

¾ cup extra virgin olive oil
2 racks of lamb, the eyes trimmed and cut
*   into 8 four-ounce medallions (have the*
*   butcher trim them for you)*
Salt and freshly ground pepper to taste
4 medium Idaho potatoes
¼ cup Mushroom Syrup (page 74)
1 medium tomato, peeled, seeded and diced
4 basil leaves, cut into ribbons, plus 4 sprigs
*   basil for garnish*

Heat 2 tablespoons olive oil over medium-high heat until very hot. Sear the medallions about 10 seconds per side. Remove immediately from the pan. Season with salt and pepper and set aside.

Peel and shred the potatoes. (Do not put in water.) Lightly season with salt. Pat the shredded potatoes around each lamb medallion, pressing firmly between your hands so the potatoes adhere.

In a large nonstick pan, heat ½ cup olive oil over medium-heat (add more oil if necessary for a depth of ½ inch). Add the lamb medallions and reduce heat to medium. Cook until potatoes are brown and crisp on both sides.

In a small saucepan, warm the Mushroom Syrup and whisk in the remaining 2 tablespoons olive oil. Add the tomato and basil. Season with salt and pepper.

Place one medallion on each of 4 warmed serving plates. Pour the sauce around each. Garnish with a sprig of fresh basil.

SERVES 4

TRUFFLED LAMB WITH FAVA BEAN PUREE

This dish, particularly when made with truffles, is a very special preparation and should be served at a dinner party for dear friends or in honor of a very special occasion.

> 2 large, fresh black truffles or 1½ cups dried mushrooms (morels, porcini, black trumpet or chanterelles)*
> All-purpose flour
> 1 egg
> 2 racks of lamb, the eyes trimmed and about 1 pound each, cut into 4 four-ounce loins (have the butcher trim them for you)
> Salt and freshly ground pepper to taste
> 3 pounds fava beans, shelled, or 2 cups shelled lima beans
> 2 tablespoons heavy cream
> 2 tablespoons sweet butter
> 2 cups fresh black trumpet mushrooms, washed
> 5 tablespoons hazelnut or extra virgin olive oil
> ½ cup Mushroom Syrup (page 74)

Finely chop the truffles (if using dried mushrooms, please see note below). Put the flour in a shallow bowl, the egg (lightly beaten) in another, and the chopped truffles in a third. Dip the lamb first into the flour, then the egg and then the truffles. Season with salt and pepper and set aside.

Cook the beans in boiling salted water until tender, about 1½ minutes. Drain them, then purée in a food processor or blender. Add the cream and 1 tablespoon butter and process until smooth. Season with salt and pepper and keep warm.

In a medium sauté pan, melt 1 tablespoon butter over medium-high heat. Add the fresh trumpet mushrooms and sauté until their liquid has evaporated. Season with salt and pepper and keep warm.

Heat the oven to 450 degrees. In a large sauté pan, heat 2 tablespoons oil over medium-high heat until hot. Add the lamb and sear about 10 seconds per side. Remove the lamb to an ovenproof dish, put it in the oven and roast for approximately 10 minutes (for medium doneness).

Heat the Mushroom Syrup and whisk in the remaining 3 tablespoons oil. Season with salt and pepper and keep warm.

Slice the lamb ½ inch thick and arrange on a serving plate with the bean purée. Pour the mushroom sauce over the lamb and garnish with the mushrooms.

SERVES 4

*If using dried mushrooms instead of truffles, make sure they are *very* dry and hard. Grind them in a food processor or blender until coarsely chopped (but not dust). Dip the lamb in egg (omit the flour), then coat with a thin layer of mushrooms. Allow to stand in the refrigerator for 1 hour. (The juices from the meat will slightly hydrate the mushrooms.) Proceed with the recipe.

LAMB WITH ARTICHOKES AND OLIVES

This dish reminds me of the south of France, where lamb fillets would be served in a classic Provençal "crust" of artichokes and olives.

> 4 medium artichokes
> 6 tablespoons extra virgin olive oil
> 2 tablespoons fresh lemon juice
> 1 ounce pitted black olives, chopped
> 1 cup unseasoned breadcrumbs, fresh or commercial
> 2 racks of lamb, the eyes trimmed and about 1 pound each (have the butcher trim them for you)
> 2 cups Artichoke Broth (page 76)
> 1 tablespoon fresh thyme leaves
> Salt and freshly ground pepper to taste

Prepare artichokes as directed on page 76.

Finely dice the artichoke hearts. Sauté in 2 tablespoons olive oil for 1 minute. Combine them in a medium bowl with the olives and breadcrumbs.

Cut the lamb into ½-inch-thick medallions. In a large sauté pan, heat 2 tablespoons olive oil over medium-high heat. Add the lamb and sauté until desired doneness, about 1 minute per side. Transfer to a broiler-proof pan large enough to hold them in a single layer. Season with salt and pepper and top with the olive mixture. Put under a preheated broiler until very hot, about 30 seconds. Remove from broiler and keep warm.

In a small saucepan, heat the Artichoke Broth over medium-high heat until boiling. Reduce by half. Whisk in the remaining 2 tablespoons olive oil and add the thyme leaves. Season with salt and pepper and serve with the lamb.

SERVES 4

BREAST OF PHEASANT PARMENTIER

My version of a classic Shepherd's Pie, which combines ground meat with a crust of mashed potatoes. Here the otherwise tough leg of pheasant is ground. You may substitute two 2- to 3-pound baby chickens for the pheasants. Antoine-Auguste Parmentier popularized the potato—virtually single-handedly—in the early nineteenth century. You may be sure that any dish called "Parmentier" features potatoes.

> 2 pheasants, breasts and legs removed, breasts skinned and boned
> ½ cup dry white wine
> ½ medium carrot, peeled and diced
> ½ medium onion, peeled and diced
> ½ stalk celery, diced
> 1 Bouquet Garni (page 194)
> 2 medium Idaho potatoes, peeled and quartered
> ½ cup warm milk
> ¼ cup hazelnut or extra virgin olive oil
> 1 sheet phyllo dough
> 5 tablespoons sweet butter
> 10 Brussels sprouts, leaves separated
> Salt and freshly ground pepper to taste
> 2 cups Mushroom Syrup (page 74)
> 2 tablespoons chopped chives

Heat the oven to 550 degrees.

Braise pheasant legs in oven with wine, carrot, onion, celery and Bouquet Garni. Cook until meat is tender, about 30 minutes. Grind or finely chop the leg meat and moisten it with the cooking liquid to form a paste. Discard remaining liquid and vegetables. Set the meat mixture aside.

Cook the potatoes in boiling salted water until tender when pierced with a fork, 15 to 20 minutes, and mash by hand, using a potato masher or fork. Add the milk and 2 tablespoons hazelnut oil. Mix to a purée. Season with salt and keep warm.

Cut eight 4-inch rounds from the phyllo. Make 4 stacks of 2 rounds each. Melt 2 tablespoons butter and brush the top rounds lightly. Place on a nonstick baking sheet and bake 3 to 4 minutes, until golden brown. Set aside.

Blanch the Brussels sprouts in boiling salted water until barely wilted, about 30 seconds. Drain and set aside.

In a large sauté pan, melt 3 tablespoons butter over medium-high heat. Add the pheasant breasts and sauté on both sides for 5 minutes in all. Season with salt and pepper.

Warm the Mushroom Syrup and whisk in 2 tablespoons hazelnut oil. Season with salt and pepper.

Divide the meat mixture among each of 4 warmed serving plates, spreading it into a 4-inch circle. Top with a ¼-inch layer of potato purée. Place Brussels sprouts around the outside edge of the potatoes. Top with a round of phyllo. Slice the pheasant breast and place around the plate. Sprinkle with chives and pour some of the sauce over the breast slices.

SERVES 4

SIMPLE SAUTES AND STEAMED DISHES

■

The vegetable juices, vinaigrettes, flavored oils and broths perfectly define simple cooking for me. They transform quickly sautéed and steamed meat, poultry, fish and shellfish into perfectly seasoned, luxurious dishes in practically no time.

The sautés and steamed dishes that follow take no longer than 15 minutes to prepare. Nothing could be easier at the end of a hectic day. If you have made any of the juices, vinaigrettes, flavored oils or broths ahead of time, dinner can be on the table in a matter of minutes. You might first try each sauté or steamed dish with one of the suggested "building blocks," but improvise as you like and your imagination won't disappoint you.

■

SAUTEING

STEAK

Red meat (and the thicker fishes such as monkfish, swordfish, halibut and salmon) contains muscle fiber that contracts when the meat is sautéed. After meat is sautéed, it should not be eaten immediately, but allowed to "rest" for up to 5 minutes. Even the best quality red meat can be tough if eaten immediately after cooking. The resting period allows the fibers to expand again, making a good steak even more tender. The meat will continue to cook after it has been removed from the pan.

Remember:

- When buying a steak, whether in the supermarket or from your butcher, look for a well-marbled cut. A marbled appearance is caused by streaks of white fat throughout the

Steamed shrimp, sautéed chicken breast

beef; these streaks of fat make beef more tender. A piece of red meat without marbling, no matter how fresh, will be tough. Only dark red beef is fresh. If the color is anything but dark red, pass it by.

- Never season meat before cooking! Salt and pepper will draw out the juices, leaving it dry. Season immediately after cooking, and the seasonings will be absorbed by the meat while it rests.

- When meat is quickly seared on all sides, a crust is formed that seals in juices and flavor. This makes for the best sautés. The cooking time in the sauté methods is brief, and the food finishes cooking during the resting time.

- Allow meat to rest for 5 minutes covered with aluminum foil or a plate.

STEP 1: In a sauté pan, cook 1 tablespoon of sweet butter and 1 tablespoon of olive or vegetable oil over medium-high heat until golden brown.

STEP 2: Place a 1-inch-thick steak in the pan. Do not season.

STEP 3: For medium-rare meat, cook 3 to 4 minutes per side.

STEP 4: Remove the steak from the pan and immediately season to taste with salt and freshly ground pepper. Cover with aluminum foil or a plate and let rest for 5 minutes.

SERVE WITH: Broccoli juice, Basil Vinaigrette (page 19), Paprika Oil (page 44), Mushroom Broth (page 74), or Mushroom Syrup (page 74) mixed with an equal amount of extra virgin olive oil.

VEAL SCALLOPINI

Veal, the meat of a young calf, should not be red like mature beef. When purchasing veal, look for as light a pink as you can find. If the color is anything but pale pink (sometimes called "white"), the veal is too old and will not be tender.

I find the scallopini available pre-cut in supermarkets a little too thin. Have your butcher cut the veal no thinner than ¼-inch thick.

STEP 1: In a sauté pan, cook 1 tablespoon of sweet butter and 1 tablespoon of olive or vegetable oil over medium-high heat until golden brown.

STEP 2: Place the veal in the pan. Do not season.

STEP 3: For pink veal, cook about 1 minute per side if ¼-inch thick; 2 minutes per side if ½-inch thick. If you want the veal less pink, cook 15 to 30 seconds longer per side.

STEP 4: Remove the veal from the pan and immediately season to taste with salt and freshly ground pepper. Cover with aluminum foil or a plate and let rest for 3 minutes.

SERVE WITH: Citrus Vinaigrette (page 19), Curry Vinaigrette (page 20), Horseradish Oil (page 45), any of the Bell Pepper Oils (page 53), Mushroom Broth (page 74), Mushroom Syrup (page 74) or Artichoke Broth (page 76).

CHICKEN BREAST

A boneless breast of chicken is less fibrous than beef. It does not need as long a resting time after cooking. In order to seal in the juices, cook the chicken breast over medium-high heat for 2 minutes on one side, then reduce the heat to medium-low and cook for 8 to 10 minutes on the other side. The chicken will be thoroughly cooked but still moist. One way to tell whether a chicken breast is cooked is to lift the little flap of meat (the *suprême*) on the underside. If it lifts easily, the meat should be done.

STEP 1: In a sauté pan, cook 1 tablespoon of sweet butter and 1 tablespoon of olive or vegetable oil over medium-high heat until golden brown.

STEP 2: Place a skinless, boneless half chicken breast in the pan, thick side down. Do not season.

STEP 3: Cook for 2 minutes over medium-high heat. Turn the chicken breast over, reduce the heat to medium-low and cook for 8 to 10 minutes longer, depending upon thickness.

STEP 4: Remove the chicken breast from the pan and immediately season with salt and freshly ground pepper. Cover with aluminum foil or a plate and let rest for 3 to 5 minutes.

SERVE WITH: Pineapple juice, Soy and Ginger Vinaigrette (page 18), Curry Oil (page 44), red Bell Pepper Oil (page 53) or Artichoke Broth (page 76).

PORK CHOP

Pork has a rich, satisfying flavor. Trim the meat from the bone and trim away any visible fat.

STEP 1: In a sauté pan, cook 1 tablespoon of sweet butter and 1 tablespoon of olive or vegetable oil over medium-high heat until golden brown.

STEP 2: Place a 1-inch-thick pork chop in the pan. Do not season.

STEP 3: Cook for 2 minutes over medium-high heat. Turn the pork chop over, reduce the heat to medium-low and cook for 7 minutes longer.

STEP 4: Remove the pork from the pan and immediately season with salt and freshly ground pepper. Cover with aluminum foil or a plate and let rest for 5 minutes.

SERVE WITH: Juniper Vinaigrette (page 21), Peanut Vinaigrette (page 21), Cumin Oil (page 44), Ginger Oil (page 44), Mustard Oil (page 44), Mushroom Broth (page 74) or Mushroom Syrup (page 74).

FISH

In France, a young chef is taught to examine fresh fish scrupulously, both at the market and when it arrives at the restaurant. In New York, I try to visit the Fulton Fish Market at least once every two weeks, early in the day (3:00 or 4:00 A.M.), to examine the fish and shellfish purchased by my supplier.

Fish is never fresher than when it is whole. In purchasing whole fish, look for these signs:

- A fish stall and its produce should have a briny, fresh smell. Fish that has a pronounced "fishy" odor has been out of the sea too long.

- The eyes of the fish should be bright, clear, and bulging, not cloudy or sunken. If the eyes are concave, rather than rounded, the fish is not fresh.

- The gills should be bright red, never brownish.

- The flesh of the fish should be firm, not soft or mushy.

If you are buying fillets, try to purchase them directly from a fishmonger, avoiding prepackaged fish whenever possible. Again, fillets—even prepackaged—should not have a strong odor and should be firm to the touch.

To sauté fish properly, you must be careful not to dry it out. In my early days at L'Auberge de l'Ill, I was taught that coating the fish before sautéing will not only give it wonderful flavor but ensure that it stays moist.

Bear in mind for both thin fish (flounder, sole, red snapper, salmon fillet and black bass) and thick fish (halibut, monkfish, salmon and swordfish steaks):

- Never season the fish before cooking. Seasoning will draw the juices out during cooking and the result will be tough, chewy fish.

- For thin fish, use one of the four methods on page 97 to make a crust to seal in moisture and flavor. Season immediately after cooking. Let the fish rest, covered, for 1 to 2 minutes.

- For thick fish, no crust is necessary as the fish is thick enough to retain moisture. Season immediately after cooking. Let the fish rest, covered, for 3 minutes.

- When fish is perfectly cooked, it is translucent on the inside and moist throughout. Doneness is really a matter of taste. Americans have been taught to cook fish until it flakes. To me, that means the fish is slightly overcooked. Prepare fish to suit yourself.

THIN FISH (FLOUNDER, SOLE, BLACK BASS, RED SNAPPER, SALMON FILLET)

Both Escoffier and Alibab, two of the greatest lions of French cooking, teach that a simple coating protects delicate fish against moisture loss. I like four simple methods of coating fish.

- A flour coating (a technique known as *meunière*, after the French word for miller).

- An egg wash.

- Potato flakes. Instant potato flakes, believe it or not, provide an interesting foil for the delicate nature of fish.

- The skin of the fish, left on one side of the fillet. Ask your fishmonger to fillet the fish this way for you.

Following Pages, from left to right: Roast beef with Chive Oil, poached salmon with Basil Oil, red snapper in Mixed Vegetable Broth, pork chop with Paprika Oil. Flavored oils, in bottles, *from left to right*: Basil, Chive and Paprika Oil.

MEUNIERE

STEP 1: Dip 1 large or 2 medium fillets in all-purpose flour. Gently shake off any excess so only a thin coating remains.

STEP 2: In a sauté pan, cook 1 tablespoon of sweet butter and 1 tablespoon of extra virgin olive oil over medium-high heat until golden brown.

STEP 3: Place the fish in the pan (do not season) and sauté for the following times:

SOLE: 1 minute 15 seconds per side.
SALMON FILLET, FLOUNDER, BLACK BASS, RED SNAPPER: 1 minute per side.

If the fillet is very thin, less than ¼ inch, the cooking time will be a few seconds less than indicated. If the fish is thicker, cook a few seconds longer.

STEP 4: Remove the fish from the pan and immediately season to taste with salt and freshly ground pepper.

STEP 5: Let the fish rest for 1 to 2 minutes (for salmon, 2 to 3 minutes). It isn't necessary to cover the fish.

EGG WASH AND POTATO FLAKES

STEP 1: In a sauté pan, cook 1 tablespoon of sweet butter and 1 tablespoon of extra virgin olive oil over medium-high heat until golden brown.

STEP 2: Egg Wash: Beat 1 egg and 1 tablespoon of water with a whisk or fork. Dip 1 large or 2 medium fillets in the egg. Let any excess egg drip off so only a thin coating remains.

Potato Flakes: Coat each fillet with a thin layer of potato flakes. Press the flakes into the flesh of the fish. Gently shake off any excess so only a thin coating remains.

STEP 3: Place the fish in the pan (do not season) and sauté for the times given on page 97.

STEP 4: Let the fish rest for 1 to 2 minutes (for salmon, 2 to 3 minutes). It isn't necessary to cover the fish.

SKIN

Leaving the skin on one side of a fillet provides the most natural protection against loss of moisture, and adds the luxurious flavor of the sea.

STEP 1: Sauté the fish, skin side first, in sweet butter and oil as for meunière. Remove from pan.

STEP 2: Season and let rest for the recommended times.

THICK FISH (HALIBUT, SALMON AND SWORDFISH STEAKS, MONKFISH)

STEP 1: In a sauté pan, cook 1 tablespoon of sweet butter and 1 tablespoon of extra virgin olive oil over medium-high heat until golden brown.

STEP 2: Reduce the heat to medium. Place the fish (1 inch thick) in the pan and cook 3 to 4 minutes per side. (Monkfish, being the thickest, will need a full 4 minutes per side.)

STEP 3: Remove the fish from the pan and immediately season with salt and freshly ground pepper. Cover with aluminum foil or a plate and let rest for 3 minutes.

The fish sautés marry perfectly with many of the vegetable juices, vinaigrettes, flavored oils and—especially—the broths. Try fish with asparagus or fennel juice, Citrus Vinaigrette (page 19), Orange-Basil Oil (page 48), Shallot Broth (page 74) or Endive Broth (page 75).

SHELLFISH

Lobster, shrimp and scallops are favorites both in France and the United States. There are some simple rules to follow:

LOBSTER: While most people seem to want lobster in the spring and, especially, summer, lobsters taste their best in late fall and early winter—October, November and December—after the lobster moults in the summer or early fall.

Buy only live lobsters. Wrap the lobster loosely in wet newspaper to keep it moist.

One-and-a-half-pound lobsters, about 5 to 6 years old, are ideal. They are large enough to be sweet, but not so old as to be tough. Occasionally a very large lobster will be sweet and tender, but you can't count on it.

Female lobsters are more tender than males and their roe enhances flavor. You can tell the sex of a lobster: In the male, the first little appendages at the base of the tail (toward the head) are hard, while those of the female are rather soft.

SCALLOPS: In France, fresh scallops can be purchased at the market in their shells, with the rosy orange coral still attached. Scallops in the shell are virtually impossible to find in the United States. That is a pity, because the roe is delicious. When buying scallops, make sure they are firm, translucent and, above all, sweet-smelling.

SHRIMP: Shrimp should not smell "fishy" if they are fresh. Fresh, uncooked shrimp, in the shell or peeled, should be light gray. If the shrimp are blackened, or if they are soft, they are not fresh enough.

SHELLFISH

For a quick sauté, sea scallops and shrimp are perfect, the fastest of all sautés. When sautéed, shellfish requires no resting time.

SHRIMP (¾ POUND MEDIUM SHRIMP SERVES 2)

Shrimp may be sautéed peeled or in the shell. If sautéing medium shrimp in the shell, add 30 seconds to the cooking time.

STEP 1: In a sauté pan, cook 1 tablespoon of sweet butter and 1 tablespoon of extra virgin olive oil over medium-high heat until golden brown.

STEP 2: Place the shrimp in the pan. Sauté over medium-high heat 45 to 60 seconds per side (1½ minutes per side for large shrimp, 2 minutes per side for jumbo).

STEP 3: Remove the shrimp from the pan and immediately season with salt and freshly ground pepper.

SERVE WITH: Carrot, zucchini, leek, broccoli or asparagus juices, any of the herb vinaigrettes, Curry Vinaigrette (page 20), Lobster or Shrimp Vinaigrette (page 22), Ginger Oil (page 44), Curry Oil (page 44) or any of the broths (try Lemon Grass Broth page 146).

You can also merely add a little extra virgin olive oil, thyme and minced garlic to the pan after the shrimp have been removed. Heat for 30 seconds and pour over the shrimp.

SEA SCALLOPS
(¾ POUND SERVES 2)

Cut the scallops so that they are approximately (but no thinner than) ½ inch thick. Some sea scallops are smaller than others and may be left whole. Lightly pat dry.

STEP 1: In a sauté pan, cook 1 tablespoon sweet butter and 1 tablespoon extra virgin olive oil over medium-high heat until golden brown.

STEP 2: Lightly coat the scallops with all-purpose flour (meunière) or leave them plain.

STEP 3: Place the scallops in the pan. Do not season. Sauté 30 seconds per side.

STEP 4: Remove the scallops from the pan and immediately season with salt and freshly ground pepper.

My favorite seasoning is just a little minced fresh garlic and some fresh thyme cooked in the butter and oil after the scallops are removed from the pan.

SERVE WITH: A vegetable juice, such as Zucchini Juice Sauce with Thyme (page 2), any herb vinaigrette or herb oil, or any of the broths. Finally, try the Mustard Wine Sauce (page 193).

STEAMING

Steaming is a perfect way to simply cook poultry, fish and shellfish. It cooks rapidly without robbing the food of its juices. In the restaurant kitchen I use a traditional Chinese bamboo basket steamer. You can use any form of steamer, whether purchased or improvised.

Cooking with steam means rapid cooking with intense heat. I have devised a method of protecting the fish or whatever I want to steam by wrapping it in plastic wrap before placing it in the steamer. This prevents direct contact with steam and creates a gentle "second steaming" within the plastic. The wrapping saves all the cooking juices. I use a plastic wrap formulated for use in microwave ovens—it is specially made to withstand high temperatures. Shrimp does very well with or without the protection of plastic wrap. As you see from the chart of steaming times that follows, shrimp cook more quickly without the plastic.

Steaming works best when the food to be cooked—shrimp, fish steaks, whatever—is arranged in a single layer. Don't stack scallops, for example; instead, arrange them in a flat package. You may scatter a small quantity of half-cooked cut-up vegetables over the food in the package. The vegetables will finish cooking at the same time.

STEAMING IN PLASTIC WRAP

STEP 1: Tear off a square of plastic wrap large enough to hold the food in a flat package. Place the food on the plastic.

STEP 2: Flavor the food with a scattering of fresh herbs and 1 tablespoon of sweet butter or extra virgin olive oil. Do not season with salt and pepper as this will draw moisture from the food.

STEP 3: Wrap the contents securely into a flat package. Place the package in a steamer set over rapidly boiling water and cover.

STEP 4: Steam for the time given in the recipe, or use the guide that follows.

STEP 5: Carefully unwrap the package. (Scissors or a sharp knife will make opening the hot package easier.)

STEP 6: Season immediately after steaming.

SERVE WITH: Any of the juices, vinaigrettes, flavored oils or broths.

THICK FISH (1 inch thick)	
Halibut	7 minutes
Monkfish, Swordfish and	
Salmon Steaks	10 minutes
SEA SCALLOPS	7 to 8 minutes
SHRIMP	
Medium	5 to 7 minutes
Large	8 minutes
Jumbo	10 minutes
BONELESS HALF CHICKEN BREAST	15 minutes

STEAMING WITHOUT PLASTIC WRAP (SHRIMP ONLY)

STEP 1: Arrange 6 large shrimp in a single layer in a steamer over rapidly boiling water and cover.

STEP 2: Steam for 1½ minutes.

STEP 3: Remove shrimp from the steamer and let rest 30 seconds. For shrimp more well done, cover before the resting period.

PHYLLO

■

Phyllo dough is an amazing alternative to the flaky puff pastry, *pâte feuilletée*, that is a staple of French cuisine. *Pâte feuilletée* is somewhat complicated to make, combining a pastry base with large quantities of butter, and it takes about six hours to prepare.

Phyllo dough is made from only flour and water. It is light and very crisp. Though you won't want to make it at home, it is inexpensive, easy to find and ready to use immediately. It can be purchased in most supermarkets and specialty shops and comes tightly wrapped with about 20 sheets of dough per box.

The phyllo dough recipes that follow can be completed in less than 30 minutes. It is important to remember that, once unwrapped, phyllo dough dries out quickly. Always cover phyllo with a damp kitchen towel when not working with it, and rewrap any unused dough tightly and store it in the refrigerator.

Phyllo is very delicate, but easily mended. Don't worry if it tears while you are working with it. Just match the torn edges, press them together and proceed with the recipe.

You can make these recipes, up to a point, ahead of time. Prepare any fillings and the like in advance, but assemble the dish at the last minute. This will ensure that the phyllo is perfectly crisp.

I use phyllo dough in various ways:

■ TO WRAP FOODS IN THE FASHION OF BEEF WELLINGTON OR IN LITTLE PACKAGES OR "PURSES."

■ TO MAKE STRUDEL-LIKE DISHES.

■ TO MAKE TRIANGULAR APPETIZERS (I THINK OF THEM AS "BRICKS") AND SIDE DISHES, AND TARTS.

Salmon Leaves with Rosemary Oil (page 108)

HOW TO WORK WITH PHYLLO DOUGH

Unwrap only the number of sheets of dough called for in the recipe. (Make sure frozen dough has thawed entirely before separating sheets. If they are still partially frozen, they will be very brittle.) Trim to the desired shape and size. Keep phyllo not in use covered with plastic wrap or a damp kitchen towel while completing the recipe. Tightly rewrap extra dough and store it in the refrigerator.

Bake unfilled phyllo dough in a 400- to 450-degree oven, as called for in the recipe, and adjust the oven rack to the lowest position. You need not grease a pan for any of the phyllo dough recipes, but a nonstick baking sheet is useful.

SALMON LEAVES WITH ROSEMARY OIL

This dish combines the soft texture of salmon with the crunch of phyllo. It is a perfect summer appetizer.

8 sheets phyllo dough, cut into 10-inch rounds
8 sprigs fresh rosemary
⅓ cup Rosemary Oil (page 47)
1 pound boneless salmon fillet, very thinly sliced
Salt and freshly ground pepper to taste

Heat the oven to 450 degrees. Adjust the oven rack to the lowest position.

Brush one round of phyllo lightly with Rosemary Oil. Sprinkle with leaves from one sprig of rosemary. Cover with a second round of phyllo and press down lightly. Repeat with the remaining rounds of phyllo. Place the rounds, not overlapping, on nonstick baking sheets. Bake until golden brown, about 5 minutes.

Cover four 10-inch ovenproof plates with layers of sliced salmon. Brush with Rosemary Oil. Set under a preheated broiler, 6 to 8 inches from the heat, and cook for 1 minute. Season with salt and pepper. Place one phyllo round on top of each plate and garnish with a sprig of rosemary.

SERVES 4

ALSATIAN TART

This is a lighter version of a traditional Alsatian dish I grew up with. I have looked for—but never found—an American substitute for *fromage blanc*, the white cheese my mother made every day from raw milk. The following method for *fromage blanc* is simple, inexpensive and works beautifully!

>   4 sheets phyllo dough, cut into 10-inch
>   rounds
>   2 tablespoons sweet butter plus 2 teaspoons
>   melted butter
>   ½ cup sliced onion
>   3 slices bacon, cut across into very thin slices
>   ¼ of 1 egg yolk
>   ½ cup Fromage Blanc (right)
>   2 tablespoons sour cream
>   Salt and freshly ground pepper to taste

Heat the oven to 400 degrees. Adjust the oven rack to the lowest position.

Stack the phyllo rounds and brush the top round with melted butter. Place on a nonstick baking sheet and bake for 5 minutes. Turn over and bake for 3 minutes longer. Set aside.

In a medium sauté pan, melt the butter over medium-high heat. Add onion and sauté un-til caramelized. Remove onion and set aside. Add the bacon to the pan and cook until crisp. Drain and set aside.

Mix together the egg yolk, *Fromage Blanc*, sour cream, salt and pepper. Spread evenly over the phyllo. Sprinkle with bacon and onion. Bake for 10 minutes.

MAKES 1 TART

FROMAGE BLANC

>   4 cups milk
>   2 tablespoons fresh lemon juice
>   Cheesecloth

Bring the milk to a rolling boil, then take it off the heat.

Stir in the lemon juice. The milk will immediately curdle, separating into whey and white *fromage blanc*. Cover the pot and leave it at room temperature for 2 hours or until cool.

Strain through a double thickness of cheesecloth, pressing out all the liquid.

Store *fromage blanc*, tightly covered, in the refrigerator up to 1 week.

MAKES 1½ TO 2 CUPS

SHRIMP, TOMATO AND CILANTRO TART

This dish also works well with fresh sea scallops or crab. Use about ½ pound of either instead of the shrimp.

> 4 sheets phyllo dough, cut into 10-inch
>   rounds
> 1 cup sliced scallions
> 2 tablespoons Lobster Oil (page 49) or
>   Shrimp Oil (page 50)
> 8 large shrimp, peeled and deveined
> 2 tablespoons peeled, seeded and diced
>   tomato
> ¼ teaspoon chopped fresh ginger
> ½ teaspoon chopped cilantro

Heat the oven to 400 degrees. Adjust the oven rack to the lowest position.

Stack the phyllo rounds and brush the top round with Lobster Oil. Place on a nonstick baking sheet and bake for 5 minutes. Turn over and bake for 3 minutes longer. Set aside.

Sauté the scallions in the remaining Lobster Oil until soft. Combine the remaining ingredients in a bowl and add the scallions and oil. Stir well to coat the shrimp and spread over the oiled surface of the phyllo tart. Bake for 10 minutes.

MAKES 1 TART

Shrimp, Tomato and Cilantro Tart

TOMATO AND BASIL TART

This Provençal inspiration combines fresh tomatoes, garlic and basil on a crisp phyllo base. Unless you are fortunate enough to have flavorful, juicy tomatoes year-round, prepare this only in the summer months when tomatoes are at their best.

4 sheets phyllo dough, cut into 10-inch rounds

2 tablespoons extra virgin olive oil

3 medium tomatoes

½ teaspoon chopped chili pepper

½ teaspoon chopped garlic

½ teaspoon chopped thyme leaves

Salt, freshly ground pepper and sugar to taste

1 tablespoon basil leaves, cut into ribbons

1 tablespoon freshly grated hard goat cheese or Parmesan

Heat the oven to 400 degrees. Adjust the oven rack to the lowest position.

Stack the phyllo rounds and brush the top round with olive oil. Place on a nonstick baking sheet and bake for 5 minutes. Turn over and bake for 3 minutes longer. Set aside.

Blanch tomatoes in boiling salted water for about 5 seconds. Remove the skins and squeeze out the liquid and seeds. Dice the tomatoes. In an ovenproof pan, combine the tomatoes, chili pepper, garlic, thyme and 1 tablespoon olive oil. Season with salt, pepper and a pinch of sugar. Bake until the tomatoes begin to turn brown and caramelize, stirring occasionally, about 20 minutes. Set aside.

Spread the tomatoes over the oiled surface of the phyllo tart. Top with basil, cheese and remaining olive oil. Bake for 10 minutes.

MAKES 1 TART

DUCK BRICKS

A phyllo package keeps the flavor of the aromatic contents within the pastry until the moment the crust is broken.

3 tablespoons sweet butter
3 ounces fresh cèpes or white button mush-
     rooms, washed and cut into small dice
¼ pound boneless duck
½ skinless, boneless half chicken breast
9 ounces uncooked foie gras or duck or
     chicken livers
1 ounce prosciutto
Salt and freshly ground pepper to taste
1 egg
3 sheets phyllo dough, cut into twelve 4 ×
     16-inch strips
2 tablespoons Truffle Vinaigrette (page 22)
     or Soy and Ginger Vinaigrette (page 18)

Heat the oven to 450 degrees. Adjust the oven rack to the lowest position.

In a small sauté pan, melt 1 tablespoon butter over medium-high heat. Add the mushrooms and sauté until golden brown. Set aside and keep warm.

Cut the duck, chicken, foie gras and prosciutto into small dice and mix together. Season with salt and pepper. Add the egg and mushrooms and mix well.

Arrange the phyllo in 4 stacks of 3 strips. Melt the remaining 2 tablespoons butter. Brush the top strips lightly with melted butter. Mound one-fourth of the duck mixture at the end of each stack of phyllo strips. Roll phyllo up and over the stuffing to form a triangle. Brush with melted butter. Place on a nonstick baking sheet and bake until golden brown, about 10 minutes.

Place 1 brick on each of 4 warmed serving plates and serve with Truffle Vinaigrette.

SERVES 4

Duck Bonbons: You will need 4 sheets of phyllo to make 18 bonbons. Heat the oven and prepare the filling as above. Cut each sheet of phyllo into 9 rectangles, 4½ × 3 inches. Make the bonbons: Stack 2 rectangles and lightly brush the top strip with melted butter. Place 1 tablespoon filling at the center edge of one long side of the rectangle. Roll the dough over the filling to enclose it completely. Gently twist the ends of the dough in opposite directions to make a "bonbon" package. Lightly brush with melted butter. Bake bonbons 5 to 7 minutes, until golden brown. Serve as above.

Following Pages: Squab Purses (page 118), Duck Bonbons, Goat Cheese Bricks with Endive Salad (page 116). Shown in bottles, *from left to right:* Chive Oil, Truffle Vinaigrette, Soy Vinaigrette.

GOAT CHEESE BRICKS WITH ENDIVE SALAD

*1 cup crumbled soft, white goat cheese such
   as Montrachet*
1½ teaspoons chopped rosemary
1½ teaspoons chopped thyme
*3 sheets phyllo dough, cut into twelve 4 ×
   16-inch strips*
*2 tablespoons extra virgin olive oil or
   Rosemary Oil (page 47)*
Endive Salad (right)

Heat the oven to 450 degrees. Adjust the oven rack to the lowest position.

Mix the cheese and herbs. Roll the mixture into four 2-inch balls. Cover and refrigerate until ready to use.

Arrange the phyllo in 4 stacks of 3 strips. Brush the top strips lightly with olive oil. Place a ball of cheese on the end of each stack of phyllo strips. Roll phyllo up and over the cheese to form a triangle. Brush tops with olive oil. Place on a nonstick baking sheet and bake until golden brown, about 10 minutes. Serve with Endive Salad.

SERVES 4

ENDIVE SALAD

3 heads endive
½ teaspoon fresh lemon juice
2 tablespoons peanut oil
2 teaspoons sherry vinegar
2 teaspoons cracked raw peanuts*
1 teaspoon chopped chives
Salt and freshly ground pepper to taste

Separate the endive leaves and slice into long, thin strips. Combine remaining ingredients in a bowl and mix well. Pour over endives and toss.

SERVES 4

*To crack peanuts, simply whack with the bottom of a heavy pot.

LAMB WITH WILD MUSHROOMS

My version of a lamb Wellington. Wrap the meat in phyllo just before cooking to ensure the crust is crisp.

> 3 cups assorted fresh wild mushrooms (shiitakes, chanterelles, morels)
> ½ teaspoon chopped garlic
> ½ teaspoon chopped shallot
> 3 tablespoons sweet butter
> 2 tablespoons chopped parsley
> Salt and freshly ground pepper to taste
> 2 one-pound lamb loins
> 2 tablespoons canola oil
> 3 sheets phyllo dough, trimmed to 10 × 13½-inch rectangles
> ½ cup Mushroom Syrup (page 74)
> 2 tablespoons hazelnut or extra virgin olive oil

Heat the oven to 450 degrees. Adjust the oven rack to the lowest position.

Wash and finely chop mushrooms. In a medium sauté pan, melt 1 tablespoon butter over medium-high heat. Add the garlic and shallot and sauté until translucent. Add the mushrooms and cook until their liquid evaporates. Add parsley and season with salt and pepper. Set aside.

In a large pan, heat the canola oil over high heat. Add the lamb and sear 3 minutes per side.

Make 2 stacks of 3 sheets phyllo each. Melt the remaining 2 tablespoons butter and brush the top sheets lightly. Divide the mushroom mixture between the top sheets and spread it evenly, leaving a 1-inch border on all sides. Roll each lamb loin in the phyllo. Pinch the ends to enclose the mixture. Roast for 10 minutes for rare, 12 minutes for medium-rare.

In a small saucepan, warm the Mushroom Syrup over medium-high heat. Whisk in the hazelnut oil and season with salt and pepper. Slice the lamb about 1 inch thick and serve with the sauce.

SERVES 4

SQUAB PURSE

4 tablespoons sweet butter

4 squab*, skinned and breasts boned

8 shiitake mushrooms

Salt and freshly ground pepper to taste

4 two-ounce slices uncooked foie gras, diced

12 sheets phyllo dough, cut into 24 eight-inch rounds

3 tablespoons hazelnut or extra virgin olive oil

½ cup Mushroom Syrup (page 74)

Heat the oven to 450 degrees. Adjust the oven rack to the lowest position.

In a large sauté pan, melt 2 tablespoons butter over medium-high heat. Add the squab and sauté 5 minutes per side. Cut each breast in 6 equal pieces. Cut mushrooms into pieces the same size as the breast meat.

Add 1 tablespoon butter to the pan and sauté the mushrooms until their liquid evaporates. Season with salt and pepper. Combine the sliced breast meat, mushrooms and foie gras in a bowl.

Arrange the phyllo in 8 stacks of 3 rounds each. Melt the remaining tablespoon butter and brush over the tops of the stacks. Divide the mushroom mixture among the stacks, mounding it in the center of each. Place one squab leg on top of each. Gather the sides of each round up to the center, to form a "purse" with the leg bone peeking out the top. Secure the purses with kitchen string.

Place on a nonstick baking sheet and brush with hazelnut oil. Bake for 15 minutes.

In a small saucepan, warm the Mushroom Syrup over medium-high heat. Whisk in 2 tablespoons hazelnut oil. Season with salt and pepper.

Put 2 purses on each of 4 warmed serving plates. Serve with the sauce.

SERVES 4

*You can substitute two 2- to 3-pound baby chickens for the squab. Slice all the meat into smallish pieces and add to the mushrooms. Remember to keep phyllo covered when not working with it, so it doesn't dry out.

LOBSTER STRUDEL

The filling can be prepared ahead of time, but to keep the phyllo crisp, assemble and bake the strudel just before serving.

> *1½-pound lobster*
> *½ cup peeled, seeded and diced tomato*
> *¼ cup chopped cilantro*
> *½ cup Lobster Oil (page 49) or Shrimp Oil (page 50)*
> *Salt and freshly ground pepper to taste*
> *3 sheets phyllo dough, trimmed to 8 × 12½-inch rectangles*

Heat the oven to 450 degrees. Adjust the oven rack to the lowest position.

Cook the lobster in boiling salted water for 2 minutes. Drain, let cool and remove the meat from the tail and claws. Dice the lobster meat and add the tomato, cilantro, 2 tablespoons Lobster Oil, salt and pepper.

Stack the phyllo sheets and brush the top sheet lightly with Lobster Oil. Spread the lobster mixture evenly over the phyllo, leaving a ½- to ¾-inch border. Starting from one long side, roll the phyllo over the filling, jelly roll fashion, and brush the top of the roll with Lobster Oil. Place the roll on a nonstick baking sheet and bake for 15 minutes. Cut into 1-inch slices and serve with the remaining Lobster Oil.

SERVES 4

APPLE TART

> *1 sheet phyllo dough, cut into four 6-inch rounds*
> *1 apple, peeled and thinly sliced*
> *3 tablespoons sweet butter, melted*
> *1 tablespoon sugar*

Heat the oven to 400 degrees. Adjust the oven rack to the lowest position.

Stack the phyllo rounds and brush the top round with butter. Place on a nonstick baking sheet and bake for 5 minutes.

Starting at the outside edge of the round, cover the phyllo with overlapping apple slices, arranging them in a spiral as you progress toward the center.

Drizzle 2 tablespoons butter over the apples. Sprinkle with sugar and bake for 15 minutes. Serve hot.

MAKES 1 TART

FOIE GRAS

■

Foie gras, the liver of a fattened goose or duck, is one of the most exquisite foods imaginable, both in flavor and in its silken texture. If calves' liver is what comes to mind when you hear the words *foie gras*, banish the thought; they don't resemble each other in the least. The delicacy of foie gras requires simple preparation so as not to overwhelm the very qualities that make it so luxurious. Traditionally it is combined or eaten with such rich flavors as those of Port, Madeira and Sauternes, in small amounts that embellish but don't compete.

Foie gras is not a dish for every day. It is expensive and, unfortunately, not the best for one's diet. But when I want to splurge, I can't think of anything I would rather eat.

Cold, freshly cooked foie gras (page 122) is the purest form of foie gras. When it is served, that purity should be maintained. It is best served with only toasted brioche or other good bread.

When preparing warm foie gras, an important step in finishing the sauce is adding back some of the fat the foie gras gave up when it was sautéed. This makes for a glossier, more richly flavored sauce.

Foie gras is certainly not to be found in every butcher shop. If you find it difficult to get fresh foie gras locally, you can order it from D'Artagnan in New Jersey, telephone 201-792-0748.

From my earliest days, watching Paul Haeberlin of L'Auberge de l'Ill prepare foie gras and tasting the result of my master's work, I have tried to create different and new dishes of foie gras. Once you start working with foie gras, you will be amazed how easy the recipes are to prepare. I hope you truly enjoy the glorious results.

Foie gras: uncooked, in milk, and Cooked Foie Gras (page 122)

COOKED FOIE GRAS

This must be prepared 1 day in advance in order for the flavor to develop properly. Let it come to room temperature before serving.

Don't use a terrine mold that is too large for the amount of foie gras to be cooked. If you have only a small amount of foie gras, use a small casserole or even a ramekin. The foie gras should be at least 2 inches thick.

> *2-pound uncooked foie gras*
> *Milk or water*
> *Pinch freshly ground pepper*
> *1 tablespoon salt*

Heat the oven to 350 degrees.

Soak the foie gras in milk or water to cover for 2 hours at room temperature. Drain it, remove the nerves and separate into 2 lobes. Season with salt and pepper.

Place the foie gras in a 1½-quart ceramic terrine mold and gently press to fill any air spaces. Cover with aluminum foil. Place the mold in a deep baking pan. Pour hot water into the baking pan to reach three-fourths up the mold. Bake for about 1 hour. To test if foie gras is done, insert a meat thermometer into the foie gras. If it reads 150 degrees, the foie gras is done. If not, continue to bake a little longer and test again. Remove the baking pan from oven and let the mold cool in the water. When it reaches room temperature, cover tightly and refrigerate.

SERVES 15

POACHED FOIE GRAS WITH FENNEL AND CARAMEL PEPPER

This is a recipe we developed at Lafayette and it is one of my favorites. As the "correct" wine to drink with foie gras is Sauternes, this dish boasts a perfect balance.

> 2 medium bulbs fennel, sliced (2 cups), leaves reserved for garnish
>
> 1 cup water
>
> 1 tablespoon sweet butter
>
> Salt to taste
>
> 4 five-ounce slices uncooked foie gras (each about ½ inch thick)
>
> 1 bottle Sauternes, Gewürztraminer or Muscat
>
> 2 tablespoons sugar
>
> ½ teaspoon cracked black pepper
>
> 4 teaspoons fresh lime juice (or to taste)

In a medium saucepan, combine the fennel, water and butter. Add a pinch of salt and cook over medium-high heat until all the water evaporates. Set aside and keep warm.

Put the foie gras in a sauté pan at least 10 inches wide and add Sauternes to cover. Poach over low heat (do not let it come to a boil) until Sauternes begins to simmer; cook for 2 minutes. Remove the foie gras and keep warm. Reserve the cooking liquid.

In a separate pan, melt the sugar with the pepper over medium-high heat and cook until it turns a rich brown color. Deglaze the pan with half the reserved cooking liquid. Reduce by half. Add the lime juice.

Put some of the fennel on each of 4 warmed serving plates. Top it with a slice of foie gras and pour some of the caramel sauce on top. Garnish with fennel leaves.

SERVES 4

MARBLE OF FOIE GRAS

This is a great party dish. One night at Lafayette a portion of warm foie gras came back to the kitchen. We didn't want to waste it and so it was placed in the refrigerator. We tasted it the following day and found the flavor to be fabulous.

This "marble" is unusual in that it uses cooked foie gras to make a cold terrine. It is simple, easily prepared when the mold is lined with plastic wrap. If you want to use only 1 pound of foie gras, divide all ingredients in half and use an accordingly smaller mold.

> 2-pound uncooked foie gras
> 2 tablespoons paprika
> Salt and freshly ground pepper to taste
> 4 cups Mushroom Broth (page 74)
> 2 tablespoons unflavored gelatin
> ¼ cup Cognac or brandy
> ¼ cup green peppercorns, drained and finely
>   chopped
> Corn Muffins (page 161), toasted

Slice the foie gras ½ inch thick and arrange in a single layer in a dish. Season with paprika, salt and pepper. Cover tightly and refrigerate 2 hours.

In a medium saucepan, warm the Mushroom Broth over medium-high heat. When it is hot, sprinkle with gelatin. Stir to dissolve. Bring the broth to a boil and season with salt and pepper. Remove from the heat and set aside.

Heat a large sauté pan over high heat. When the pan is hot, add the foie gras and sauté 20 seconds per side. Remove foie gras from the pan and drain the fat. Deglaze the pan with Cognac and cook until the Cognac evaporates. Add the Mushroom Broth and reduce by half. Add the chopped green peppercorns and remove from the heat.

Line a 1½-quart ceramic terrine mold with plastic wrap. Arrange a layer of the foie gras in the mold and cover with broth. Continue layering, ending with broth. Cover tightly with plastic wrap and refrigerate, weighted, until the terrine is firm, at least 4 hours. Slice about ⅓ inch thick and serve with Corn Muffins.

SERVES 12

FOIE GRAS WITH FRIED LEEKS

1-pound uncooked foie gras, cut into 4 slices
Salt and freshly ground pepper to taste
2 tablespoons sherry vinegar
2 cups Mushroom Broth (page 74)
3 tablespoons Peanut Oil (page 51) or
*   commercial peanut oil*
1 tablespoon cracked black pepper
2 tablespoons cracked raw peanuts*
2 tablespoons chopped chives

Garnish: Leek Julienne (page 197)

Heat a medium sauté pan over high heat. When the pan is hot, add the foie gras and sauté for 1½ minutes per side. Remove foie gras from the pan and place on individual plates. Season with salt and pepper and cover to keep warm.

Drain excess fat from the pan. Deglaze the pan with vinegar and cook until the vinegar evaporates. Add the Mushroom Broth and reduce to a syrup (no more than ½ cup). Whisk in the Peanut Oil (the oil will separate from the rest of the sauce). Keep warm.

Sprinkle the cracked pepper, peanuts and chives around the foie gras. Top the foie gras with fried leeks and spoon a little sauce around the plate.

SERVES 4

*To crack peanuts, give them one or two whacks with the bottom of a heavy pot.

Following Pages, clockwise from top left: Roulade of Foie Gras (page 130), Foie Gras Poached with Fennel and Caramel Pepper (page 123), Foie Gras with Fried Leeks, Sautéed Foie Gras and Potato Tureen (page 128), Soufflé of Foie Gras (page 131), Marble of Foie Gras, Foie Gras with Ginger and Mango (page 129).

SAUTEED FOIE GRAS AND POTATO TERRINE

This is a signature dish created in the fall of 1988. My former Sous-Chef Pierre Schultz always lined pans with thin slices of potatoes for this recipe.

This dish takes a little time, but it's worth it. The potato takes on the character of the foie gras, the foie gras the character of the potato. When you are comfortable with one or two of the other foie gras preparations, try this dish. You won't be disappointed.

Don't add fat to the pan before sautéing slices of terrine. The fat of the foie gras will be enough.

> 10 medium Idaho potatoes, peeled and
> sliced ⅛ inch thick
> 1 cup Clarified Butter (page 194)
> 1 pound uncooked foie gras, cut into ½-inch
> slices
> All-purpose flour
> Salt and freshly ground pepper to taste
> ½ cup Mushroom Syrup (page 74)
> ¼ cup hazelnut oil
> 2 tablespoons sherry vinegar
> ¼ cup chopped chives
> Pinch coarse salt

Heat the oven to 400 degrees.

Dip the potato slices in Clarified Butter. Arrange in a single layer on a nonstick baking sheet. Bake until tender but remove from the oven before they take on any color, about 15 minutes. Lightly pat dry with paper toweling.

Line a 1½-quart ceramic terrine mold with plastic wrap, leaving a 4-inch overhang on all sides. Line the mold with a ¼-inch layer of potatoes on the bottom and up the sides.

Place a layer of foie gras over the potatoes. Cover foie gras with another ¼-inch layer of potatoes, then add the remaining foie gras and finish with the remaining potatoes. Cover the mold with the overhang of plastic wrap. Weight the top of the mold and refrigerate for at least 2 hours.

Unmold the terrine and slice ½ inch thick. Dust the slices with flour and shake off any excess. Heat a large nonstick pan over high heat. When the pan is very hot, add the slices of terrine and sauté about 30 seconds per side, until potato is golden brown and crisp. Remove to warmed serving plates.

Warm the Mushroom Syrup and whisk in the hazelnut oil and sherry vinegar. Remove from the heat and season with salt and pepper.

Sprinkle chives around each plate. Sprinkle a pinch of coarse salt on each slice of terrine and a turn of fresh pepper from a pepper mill. Pour a little of the sauce around each plate and serve.

SERVES 12

FOIE GRAS WITH GINGER AND MANGO

The traditional Outhier warm foie gras dish combines foie gras with apples and sorrel. When I was sent to Thailand and couldn't find apples, I used mangoes instead.

2 ripe mangoes
1 tablespoon powdered sugar
4 one-and-a-half-inch slices uncooked foie gras (4 ounces each)
2 cups fresh orange juice
½ cup dry white wine
1 tablespoon fresh ginger julienne
1 teaspoon fresh lime juice
Salt and freshly ground pepper to taste

Peel the mangoes and cut the flesh away from the pits in 2 large halves each. Cut each half from the top nearly to the bottom into 4 long slices. Fan the slices. Sprinkle one side of each fan with sugar and cook, sugar side down, in a nonstick pan over medium-high heat until caramelized. Place on serving plates, caramel side up.

Heat a small sauté pan over medium-high heat until hot. Add the foie gras and cook 1½ minutes per side. Remove from the pan and keep warm. Deglaze the pan with orange juice, white wine and ginger. Reduce to a syrup and add lime juice and any fat given off by the foie gras. Season with salt and pepper. Place the foie gras next to the mango fans and spoon some of the sauce over it.

SERVES 4

FOIE GRAS WITH FIGS

This is very simple and the flavor is unique. If you want to make the roulade quickly, though, substitute good-quality prosciutto.

Air-dried Duck Breast (right) or 1 pound
    thinly sliced prosciutto
7 ounces Cooked Foie Gras (page 122),
    left at room temperature until soft
6 fresh figs
36 leaves mâche or arugula
1 teaspoon cracked black pepper
Port Wine Aspic (right)
1 tablespoon chives, cut into ½-inch lengths

Slice duck breasts very thin. Spread a sheet of aluminum foil over a kitchen surface. Arrange the sliced duck on the foil in a single layer. Spread with foie gras and roll into a cylinder. Wrap in the foil and twist the ends tightly. Refrigerate until firm, about 2 hours.

Slice roulade and the figs approximately ¼ inch thick. Alternate three slices of each on serving plates. Garnish with mâche leaves. Scatter the pepper, aspic and chives over all.

SERVES 6

AIR-DRIED DUCK BREAST

1-pound whole duck breast, skinned
6 coriander seeds, cracked
1 bay leaf
1 bunch thyme
1 tablespoon coarse salt
6 black peppercorns

Rub the duck breast with the remaining ingredients, cover loosely and let sit for 24 hours. Hang it in cheesecloth in a cool, well-ventilated place to cure for 15 days.

PORT WINE ASPIC

1 bottle port wine
1½ tablespoons unflavored gelatin

Heat the port until hot. Sprinkle the gelatin over the port and stir to dissolve thoroughly. Pour into a jelly roll pan and refrigerate until firm, about 1½ hours. Cut into small dice.

SOUFFLE OF FOIE GRAS

This dish is fabulously rich and needs no sauce. Serve with a glass of Sauternes or Champagne.

>   1 tablespoon sweet butter
>   1 tablespoon all-purpose flour
>   4 eggs, separated
>   ¼ cup truffle juice* or slightly reduced Mushroom Broth (page 74)
>   Generous ¼ cup uncooked foie gras, for purée
>   ½ cup diced uncooked foie gras
>   Pinch salt
>   Pinch cream of tartar

Heat the oven to 500 degrees.

Butter and flour four 4-ounce ceramic ramekins and set them in the freezer.

Beat together the egg yolks and truffle juice in the top of a double broiler set over—not touching—boiling water. Whisk until light and fluffy. Let cool to room temperature.

Pass ¼ cup foie gras through a sieve to purée. Mix the purée into the egg mixture. Beat the egg whites with salt and cream of tartar until stiff. Fold gently into the foie gras mixture, then pour into each ramekin until half full. Divide the diced foie gras among the ramekins, then fill them with the remaining soufflé mixture. Place the ramekins in a deep baking dish. Add hot water to reach halfway up the ramekins. Cook for 15 minutes and serve immediately.

SERVES 4

*Available in cans from specialty stores and gourmet shops. The liquid in which canned or jarred truffles are packed may be used.

ON AN ORIENTAL NOTE

When I joined Louis Outhier's "flying squadron of chefs," a large part of my time from 1981 to 1983 was spent in the Orient: Bangkok, Hong Kong and Singapore. The flavors and subtleties of the ingredients and spices of the Far East brought a new dimension to my cooking.

The recipes that follow are a marriage of the influences of the Orient and of France. They aren't intended to be used exclusively as part of "Eastern" menus, and are exquisite with and often enhanced by Western flavors. As you will see, many of the recipes call for one or two seemingly exotic "Eastern" ingredients. All can be obtained in Oriental markets throughout the United States.

Eggs with Oysters (page 134)

EGGS WITH OYSTERS

½ cup heavy cream, whipped
½ tablespoon wasabi powder*, mixed to a
  paste with ½ tablespoon water
Salt and cayenne pepper to taste
1 tablespoon sesame seeds
2 tablespoons sweet butter
4 eggs
8 large, fresh oysters, coarsely chopped

Heat the oven to 250 degrees.

Combine the whipped cream and wasabi paste. Season with salt and cayenne pepper and mix well. Refrigerate until needed.

Spread sesame seeds on a baking sheet and bake until they are lightly toasted.

Melt 1 tablespoon butter in a small saucepan over medium-low heat. In a medium bowl, whisk together the eggs, salt and cayenne pepper. Add to the saucepan and cook, stirring constantly with a wooden spoon until eggs scramble; add the remaining 1 tablespoon butter toward the end of cooking. They should be fairly loose, not dry.

Divide the eggs among 4 ramekins. Top with chopped oysters and cover with a spoonful of wasabi cream. Sprinkle sesame seeds over the cream and serve.

SERVES 4

*Wasabi powder may be purchased in an Oriental market featuring Japanese products. It has a flavor similar to that of horseradish.

TEMPURA WITH CABBAGE SALAD AND CINNAMON OIL

3 cups shredded Chinese cabbage (about
  ¼ pound)
1 teaspoon honey
¼ cup rice vinegar
1 teaspoon cracked green coriander seeds
1 teaspoon grated lemon zest
1 teaspoon grated orange zest
1 teaspoon chopped fresh ginger
Salt and cayenne pepper to taste
2 tablespoons cornstarch
2 tablespoons water
32 large shrimp, peeled to the tail and
  deveined
1½ cups canola oil
¼ cup Cinnamon Oil (page 44)

Toss the cabbage thoroughly with honey, vinegar, coriander, zests, ginger, salt and cayenne pepper. Cover and let stand at room temperature for at least 1 hour.

Combine the cornstarch and water and mix well. In a large sauté pan or Chinese wok, heat the oil to 375 degrees. Dip shrimp into cornstarch mixture and fry until crisp, about 1 minute. Season with salt and cayenne pepper. Serve with the cabbage salad and sprinkle Cinnamon Oil over all.

SERVES 4

VEAL IN RICE PAPER

When you have used rice paper just once, you will be eager to experiment. It can be used as a wrapper for all kinds of fillings. Try sautéed foie gras and apples with Curry Oil (page 44) or chopped, uncooked shrimp with cilantro, scallions and Shrimp Oil (page 50) or Lobster Oil (page 49). Rice paper packages may be lightly fried in a small amount (1 tablespoon) of peanut or sesame oil in a nonstick pan.

> 2 tablespoons sweet butter
> 1¼ pounds veal (top round), cut into large dice
> 2 cups chanterelle or shiitake mushrooms
> 1 tablespoon finely chopped fresh ginger
> 3 tablespoons sliced scallions
> 2 tablespoons soy sauce
> 1 tablespoon fresh lemon juice
> 2 tablespoons nam pla* (fish sauce)
> Salt and freshly ground pepper to taste
> 3 tablespoons chopped cilantro
> 4 eight-inch sheets rice paper*
> ¼ cup Soy and Ginger Vinaigrette
>   (page 18), warmed

Melt the butter in a large sauté pan over medium-high heat. Add the veal and sauté until light brown, 5 to 7 minutes. Season with salt and pepper.

Wash the mushrooms and lightly pat dry. Cut any large mushrooms in half. Add mushrooms, ginger and scallions to veal. Cook until mushroom liquid evaporates, about 5 minutes.

Deglaze the pan with soy sauce, lemon juice and nam pla. Bring to a boil and remove from heat. Season with salt and pepper and stir in the cilantro.

Soften each round of rice paper between layers of damp kitchen toweling for about 5 minutes, until pliable enough to roll without cracking, but not wet. Divide the veal mixture among the rounds, mounding it in the center of each. Fold the rice paper around the mixture to form a rectangular packet. Steam packets over boiling water for 5 minutes. Serve with warm Soy and Ginger Vinaigrette.

SERVES 4

*Nam pla and rice paper are sold in Oriental markets.

THAI SHRIMP CAKES

My version of Tod Mon Pla. Nam pla is a fish sauce that can be purchased in Oriental markets.

1 stalk lemon grass, chopped

1 cup boiling water

1 pound medium shrimp, peeled and deveined

2 tablespoons sliced scallions

1 tablespoon chopped cilantro

Salt and cayenne pepper to taste

¼ cup nam pla (fish sauce)

2 tablespoons plus 2 teaspoons fresh lime juice

1 teaspoon honey

2 tablespoons cracked raw peanuts*

¼ cup cucumber, seeded and diced

1 medium chili pepper, finely chopped

2 tablespoons peanut oil, homemade or commercial

2 tablespoons sweet butter

2 tablespoons canola oil

Garnish: Sliced scallions and chopped cilantro

Put the lemon grass in a bowl and cover with boiling water. Let infuse for 10 minutes. Strain the liquid and let cool to room temperature.

In a food processor or blender, combine the shrimp with ½ cup of the infusion. Process until nearly smooth but still somewhat chunky. Transfer to a bowl and stir in scallions and cilantro. Season with salt and cayenne pepper. Set aside.

Combine the remaining ingredients except the butter, canola oil and Garnish. Set aside.

Heat the butter and canola oil in a nonstick pan over medium-high heat. Drop large tablespoonfuls of shrimp mixture into the pan and flatten them slightly into 2-inch cakes. Cook about 30 seconds per side until golden brown. Pool some of the sauce on each serving plate and top with the shrimp cakes. Garnish with scallions and cilantro.

SERVES 4

*To crack peanuts, give them one or two whacks with the bottom of a heavy pan.

RICE PAPER SUSHI

This sushi is served cold, a perfect appetizer or summer dish. The flavors come together nicely during refrigeration. It may be prepared up to 6 hours in advance, but let it sit at room temperature for 3 to 5 minutes before serving. Rounds of rice paper and wasabi powder are available at most Oriental markets. This roll reminds me of *futomaki* or a California roll.

> 2 eight-inch sheets rice paper
> ½ cup bean sprouts
> Lightly cooked seafood: ½ small lobster, 5
>   medium sea scallops, 5 medium shrimp
>   or a thin slice of cod (3 to 4 ounces)
> 2 or 3 slices avocado
> 1 tablespoon cilantro leaves
> Spiced Soy Sauce (right)

Soften each round of rice paper between layers of damp kitchen toweling for about 5 minutes until pliable enough to roll without cracking, but not wet.

Place a sheet of plastic wrap on a clean kitchen surface. Stack the softened rounds of rice paper on the plastic wrap.

Arrange bean sprouts in a line about one-third of the way across the rice paper, reaching all the way to the edges. Place the fish or shellfish over the sprouts and top with slices of avocado. Sprinkle with cilantro.

Roll the rice paper and its contents tightly into a long roll (leave the ends open). Wrap the roll tightly in plastic, twisting the ends to make an air-tight package.

Refrigerate for at least 1 hour. When ready to serve, unwrap and cut into 2-inch pieces. Serve with Spiced Soy Sauce.

SERVES 2

SPICED SOY SAUCE

> ½ cup soy sauce
> 1 teaspoon wasabi powder
> 1 tablespoon minced fresh ginger
> 1 tablespoon sake
> 1 tablespoon rice wine vinegar
> 1 tablespoon dark sesame oil or peanut oil

Combine all ingredients.

Following Pages: Thai Shrimp Cakes, Rice Paper Sushi

SWEETBREAD FRITTERS WITH GINGER VINAIGRETTE

½ pound sweetbreads
1¾ cups all-purpose flour
1½ cups plus 1 tablespoon canola oil
1 whole egg
3 tablespoons beer
¾ cup water
3 egg whites
Salt
¼ cup Ginger Vinaigrette (page 18)
2 tablespoons chopped cilantro

Put the sweetbreads in cold salted water and bring the water to a boil. Drain the sweetbreads and remove the nerves. Cut into large dice. Refrigerate until needed.

Combine flour, 1 tablespoon oil, whole egg, beer and water and mix well. Beat the egg whites with a pinch of salt to stiff peaks. Fold into the beer batter.

In a Chinese wok or large sauté pan, heat the remaining 1½ cups oil until very hot (315 degrees). Dip the diced sweetbreads into the batter. Fry about 2 minutes, until golden brown on all sides. Drain on paper toweling and sprinkle with salt.

Combine the Ginger Vinaigrette and cilantro. Serve with the sweetbread fritters.

SERVES 4

GRILLED PIG'S FEET WITH PEANUTS

Don't be put off—try this one! This Thai-inspired dish is simple and truly wonderful. To crack peanuts, give them a whack with the bottom of a heavy pot.

4 cooked pig's feet (purchase from a butcher)
2 tablespoons cracked raw peanuts
2 tablespoons unseasoned breadcrumbs, fresh or commercial
2 tablespoons peanut oil, homemade or commercial
¼ cup Dijon mustard

Put the pig's feet in a pot and add enough water to cover them halfway. Cook over medium heat for 10 minutes. Drain and remove the bones. Press the meat into espresso-size cups lined with plastic wrap. Cover tightly and refrigerate overnight.

Heat the oven to 550 degrees.

Mix together the peanuts and breadcrumbs. Carefully remove the meat from the cups and brush with oil and mustard. Roll in the breadcrumb mixture. Place on a baking sheet and bake for 20 minutes. Place under a preheated broiler until the crust browns. Serve with a mixed salad or Endive Salad (page 116).

SERVES 4

LACQUERED BACON

½ medium carrot, peeled
½ medium onion, peeled
½ medium leek, washed thoroughly
2 pounds raw, unsmoked and unsliced bacon
1 Bouquet Garni (page 194)
¼ cup honey
¼ cup vinegar (rice wine, white wine or any other white vinegar)
Honey-Ginger Glazed Shallots (right)

Cut the vegetables into large cubes. Put the vegetables, bacon and Bouquet Garni in a pot with water to cover. Bring to a boil and reduce heat. Simmer for 1 hour.

Drain the bacon and cut into large cubes. Discard the vegetables and liquid.

In a medium sauté pan, heat the honey over medium-high heat until caramelized. Deglaze the pan with vinegar. Add the bacon and cook, stirring constantly, until bacon is well coated. Serve with Honey-Ginger Glazed Shallots.

SERVES 4

HONEY-GINGER GLAZED SHALLOTS

1½ cups medium shallots, peeled and thinly sliced
2 tablespoons fresh ginger julienne
¼ cup honey
⅓ cup red wine vinegar
½ cup water
¼ teaspoon cracked black pepper
Salt to taste

In a medium saucepan, combine the shallots, ginger and honey. Cook over medium-high heat about 5 minutes, until caramelized. Deglaze the pan with vinegar and cook until the vinegar evaporates. Add the water and reduce heat to medium-low. Cook until nearly dry. Stir in the cracked pepper and season with salt.

THAI CHICKEN SOUP WITH COCONUT MILK

2 tablespoons sweet butter

¼ cup chopped onion

2 tablespoons chopped lemon grass

2 tablespoons chopped fresh ginger

½ teaspoon red pepper flakes

1 chili pepper, seeded, deribbed and chopped

4 cups Mixed Vegetable Broth (page 75)

2 whole chicken breasts, skinned and boned

2 tablespoons sliced scallions

2 tablespoons peeled, seeded and diced tomato

2 tablespoons chopped cilantro

1 cup coconut milk*

1 cup button mushrooms, cut into large dice

2 tablespoons nam pla* (fish sauce)

Salt to taste

Melt the butter in a large sauté pan over medium-high heat.

Add the onion, lemon grass, ginger, red pepper flakes and chili pepper and cook until onion is translucent. Add Mixed Vegetable Broth and cook for 10 minutes. Add chicken breasts and poach for 5 minutes. Remove the chicken and strain the liquid, discarding the solids. Cut the chicken into large dice and place in a large soup tureen. Add scallions, tomato and cilantro to the tureen.

Heat the strained liquid with the coconut milk and mushrooms and bring to a boil. Stir in nam pla and cook for 5 minutes. Season with salt. Add the broth to the tureen.

SERVES 4

*Nam pla is fish sauce that can be purchased in Oriental markets. Coconut milk is not the liquid inside coconuts. It can be found in gourmet shops and markets specializing in Latin and Oriental groceries. Be sure not to buy sweetened coconut milk or coconut cream.

SHRIMP AND CHICKEN IN LEMON GRASS BROTH

3 cups water

1 large chili pepper, seeded, deribbed and chopped

2 stalks lemon grass, chopped

2 whole chicken breasts, skinned and boned

24 medium shrimp, peeled and deveined

2 tablespoons plus 1 teaspoon nam pla* (fish sauce)

³⁄₄ cup button mushrooms, cut into small dice

¹⁄₄ cup sliced scallions

2 tablespoon chopped cilantro

¹⁄₂ teaspoon fresh lemon juice

Grated zest of ¹⁄₂ lime

In a large pot, boil the water, chili pepper and lemon grass for 10 minutes.

Cut the chicken into pieces the same size as the shrimp. Add the chicken and shrimp to the broth. Boil until done, about 5 minutes.

In a soup tureen, combine the remaining ingredients. Add the broth, chicken and shrimp to the tureen. Ladle into serving bowls over cooked white rice.

SERVES 4

*Nam pla is a fish sauce that can be purchased in Oriental markets.

WARM SHRIMP SALAD WITH BEAN SPROUTS

8 button mushrooms, cleaned and quartered

2 tablespoons fresh lemon juice

2 tablespoons plain yogurt

¹⁄₄ cup heavy cream, whipped

Salt and freshly ground pepper to taste

2 tablespoons sweet butter

24 large shrimp, peeled and deveined

1 shallot, peeled and finely chopped

3 tablespoons soy sauce

1 cup bean sprouts

2 tablespoons raw soy nuts or peanuts

3 tablespoons peanut oil

In a small bowl, combine the mushrooms, lemon juice, yogurt and whipped cream. Season with salt and pepper. Set aside.

Melt the butter in a large sauté pan over medium-high heat. Add the shrimp and sauté until half cooked, about 45 seconds per side. Add the shallot and soy sauce. Bring to a boil, remove from the heat and transfer to a bowl. Toss in the bean sprouts, soy nuts and peanut oil. Season with salt and pepper.

Arrange the mushrooms like 3 spokes on a plate. Mound the shrimp mixture between the spokes and spoon some of the cooking liquid over them.

SERVES 4

LOBSTER WITH THAI SPICES

This was one of the first Oriental dishes created by Louis Outhier, and it is still one of my favorites.

> 4 one-and-a-half-pound lobsters
> 4 tablespoons sweet butter
> ½ teaspoon shrimp paste*
> ½ teaspoon curry paste*
> ⅓ medium carrot, peeled and julienned
> ½ cup white port
> ¼ apple, peeled and julienned
> ½ teaspoon turmeric
> ¼ cup heavy cream, whipped
> 1 tablespoon chopped cilantro
> Salt and freshly ground pepper to taste

Blanch the lobsters in boiling salted water for 2 minutes. Drain. When cool enough to handle, carefully remove the meat in one piece from the claws and tails. Set aside.

Melt 2 tablespoons butter in small saucepan over medium-high heat. Add the shrimp and curry pastes and sauté 20 seconds. Add the carrot and a pinch of salt and sauté 20 seconds. Deglaze the pan with port and add the apple. Cook until almost dry. Add the turmeric and mix well. Stir in the whipped cream and bring to a boil. Remove from the heat and add cilantro and salt to taste. Keep warm.

Melt the remaining 2 tablespoons butter in a large sauté pan. Add the lobster meat and sauté for 2 minutes. Season with salt and pepper and serve napped with the sauce.

S E R V E S   4

*Shrimp and curry pastes can be purchased in Oriental markets.

Lobster with Thai Spices

LOBSTER POACHED IN LEMON GRASS BROTH

4 one-and-a-half-pound lobsters

3 cups water

2 stalks lemon grass*, coarsely chopped

½ chili pepper, seeded, deribbed and chopped

6 sprigs plus 2 tablespoons chopped cilantro

8 button mushrooms, sliced

4 scallions, sliced

2 tablespoons fresh lime juice

2 tablespoons nam pla* (fish sauce)

Blanch the lobsters in boiling salted water for 2 minutes. Drain. When cool enough to handle, remove the heads, claws and tails. Carefully remove the meat in one piece from the claws and tails. Set aside.

Put the shells and heads in a pot. Cover with water and add lemon grass, chili pepper and cilantro sprigs. Bring to a boil, reduce heat and simmer for 10 minutes. Strain into a clean saucepan.

Add the lobster meat to the strained broth with the mushrooms and scallions. Simmer for 3 minutes over medium-low heat. Stir in the lime juice, nam pla and chopped cilantro.

SERVES 4

*Nam pla is a fish sauce that can be purchased in Oriental markets. Lemon grass is also available in Oriental markets, especially those that feature Thai ingredients.

BLACK BASS IN ZUCCHINI BLOSSOMS

This dish combines the Provençal idea of a fish-stuffed zucchini blossom with the Oriental flavor of cardamom. It would be very nice served with sautéed sliced zucchini. Zucchini blossoms can be hard to find. Lettuce leaves, blanched 20 seconds in boiling salted water, may be used to wrap the fish instead.

4 six-ounce black bass fillets

Salt and cayenne pepper to taste

12 large (about 4 inches long) zucchini blossoms, pistils and stamens removed

3 cups Mixed Vegetable Broth (page 75)

2 tablespoons cracked green cardamom seeds

3 tablespoons sweet butter

2 tablespoons fresh lemon juice

Cut bass into 12 equal pieces and season with salt and cayenne pepper. Stuff a piece of fish into each blossom. Steam over boiling water for 5 minutes. Remove from the steamer and keep warm.

In a medium saucepan, bring the Mixed Vegetable Broth to a boil over medium-high heat and add cardamom seeds. Reduce to ¾ cup. Whisk in the butter and lemon juice. Season with salt and pepper. Serve over the stuffed blossoms.

SERVES 4

LACQUERED QUAIL WITH SESAME SEEDS

Sometimes the simplest dishes are the best: a perfect marriage of East and West.

> *½ cup honey*
> *½ cup soy sauce*
> *¼ scallion, sliced*
> *Freshly ground pepper to taste*
> *8 quail or 2 two- to three-pound baby chickens*
> *3 tablespoons fresh lime juice*
> *½ cup water*
> *2 tablespoons sesame seeds*
> *Spiced Rice (page 162)*

Heat the oven to 550 degrees.

Mix the honey, soy sauce, scallion and pepper. Add the quail and stir to coat. Let them marinate for 15 minutes.

Remove the quail from the marinade and roast for 12 to 15 minutes, until juices run clear (if using baby chickens, roast for 20 to 25 minutes). Reserve the marinade.

Remove quail to a broiler-proof dish. Deglaze the roasting pan with lime juice, water and ¼ cup of the marinade over medium-high heat. Reduce until the sauce is thick enough to coat a spoon. Coat the quail with sauce. Sprinkle sesame seeds over the quail and place them under a preheated broiler until piping hot; seeds should be golden brown. Serve with Spiced Rice and some of the sauce.

SERVES 4

CHICKEN WITH LIME AND HONEY

> *Zest of 1 lime, julienned*
> *5 tablespoons sweet butter*
> *1 three-pound chicken, cut into serving pieces*
> *1 tablespoon thinly sliced fresh ginger*
> *1 tablespoon honey*
> *½ cup water*
> *2 tablespoons fresh lime juice*
> *Salt and freshly ground pepper to taste*
> *2 tablespoons chopped cilantro*
> *Corn Pancakes (page 161)*

Heat the oven to 550 degrees.

Blanch the lime zest in boiling water for 10 seconds. Drain and set aside.

Melt the butter in a large oven-proof pan over medium-high heat. Add the chicken and sauté until golden brown, about 5 minutes per side. Add the ginger and honey and stir well to coat. Roast for 15 minutes until caramelized. Add the water and roast for 3 minutes longer, until juices run clear when chicken is pricked. Add the lime juice and season with salt and pepper.

Arrange the chicken on a warmed serving platter and pour the sauce on top. Sprinkle with chopped cilantro and lime zest. Serve with Corn Pancakes.

SERVES 4

POTATOES, CHEESE AND OTHER INDULGENCES

H ere you will find potatoes to suit all tastes. From my point of view, it is hard to imagine a dish that potatoes, in one form or another, won't accompany beautifully and—maybe— make even better.

Rich potatoes, crisp potatoes, exotic potatoes, I love them all. This chapter is much more than a collection of my favorite potatoes, though. Some recipes feature cheeses or vegetables, some are for unusual soups and breads. Many of the recipes are as perfect for first courses and light lunches as they are for side dishes. And, most of them are very easy.

Back to front: Wild Mushroom Gâteau (page 155), Pommes Annette (page 150), Oatmeal Pancakes (page 160), Swiss Chard Timbales (page 156).

POTATO AND BASIL PUREE

3 medium Idaho potatoes, peeled, rinsed and cut into large pieces
¾ cup milk, warmed
Salt
15 large basil leaves
6 tablespoons extra virgin olive oil

Heat the oven to 550 degrees.

Cook potatoes in boiling salted water until tender when pierced with a fork, 15 to 20 minutes. Drain potatoes and spread them out on a baking sheet. Dry in the oven for 7 to 10 minutes, until they whiten slightly and no longer look moist on the surface. Mash potatoes by hand with a potato masher or fork. Add milk and beat until smooth. Season with salt. Set aside and keep warm.

Blanch basil leaves in boiling salted water for 20 seconds. Drain and immediately refresh under cold running water. Lightly pat dry and put in a blender. Add olive oil and blend until very smooth.

Add basil purée to the potatoes and mix well. Heat thoroughly and serve.

SERVES 4

POMMES ANNETTE

4 large Idaho potatoes, peeled, rinsed and turned (trimmed in smooth ovals)
Salt
¼ cup Clarified Butter (page 194)
2 teaspoons sweet butter

Heat the oven to 550 degrees. Adjust the oven rack to the lowest position.

Slice the potatoes into coins as thin as possible. Put in a colander and sprinkle with salt. Let sit until potatoes give up some of their liquid, about 5 minutes.

Toss the potatoes in Clarified Butter to coat. Space 4 potato slices apart on a nonstick baking sheet. Fan potatoes in a circle around each of the 4 slices to make four 4-inch round "tarts." Cover the center of each with 1 final slice of potato and top each with ½ teaspoon butter. Cook until the potatoes are golden brown, about 45 minutes. Drain any excess butter and carefully transfer to warmed plates.

SERVES 4

POTATO RAVIOLI

½ cup canola oil
2 large Idaho potatoes, peeled and sliced lengthwise as thin as possible
¼ cup sweet butter
½ medium carrot, peeled and cut into small dice
½ medium turnip, peeled and cut into small dice
½ medium zucchini, cut into small dice
½ medium knob celeriac, peeled and cut into small dice
1 medium truffle, cut into small dice
Salt and freshly ground pepper to taste
4 egg yolks

Heat the oven to 400 degrees.

Lightly brush a nonstick baking sheet with canola oil. Arrange potato slices on the baking sheet in a single layer and brush with oil. Bake until tender, about 5 to 7 minutes; do not let the potatoes take on any color. Lightly pat potatoes dry with paper toweling.

Melt the butter in a medium sauté pan over medium-high heat. Add the diced vegetables and sauté until crisp-tender, about 2 minutes. Season with salt and pepper.

Beat the egg yolks. Brush one side of the potatoes lightly with egg yolk. Mound about 1 teaspoon of the diced vegetables on half of each potato and fold over to form a raviolo. Press firmly around the edges to secure. Cover and refrigerate until ready to cook.

Heat the oil until very hot (350 to 375 degrees). Add the potato ravioli and fry until golden brown on all sides, about 45 seconds. Serve hot.

SERVES 4

■

GOAT CHEESE WITH WATERCRESS OIL

This cheese makes a delicious, simple appetizer with country bread, toasted or left plain. Served with nuts and dried fruits, it's a very nice way to end a meal, too. If you like, roll the mixture into a log, then slice when it is chilled and firm.

¾ pound soft, white goat cheese (such as Montrachet)
¼ cup crème fraîche or sour cream
1 tablespoon chopped chervil
1 tablespoon chopped chives
1 chili pepper, seeded, deribbed and finely chopped
Freshly ground pepper to taste
1 tablespoon Watercress Oil (page 54)

Mix the goat cheese, crème fraîche, herbs, chili pepper and ground pepper until smooth. Shape into 4 thick patties. Cover and refrigerate until ready to use. Place on small serving plates and drizzle with Watercress Oil.

SERVES 4

MILLEFEUILLE OF ROQUEFORT AND BOURSIN

½ cup Roquefort, at room temperature
½ cup Boursin or cream cheese, at room
  temperature
1 tablespoon sweet butter
½ teaspoon Cognac or brandy
½ cup heavy cream, whipped
1 tablespoon chopped chives
Salt and freshly ground pepper to taste
3 sheets phyllo dough, trimmed to 8 × 8-inch
  squares
3 tablespoons sweet butter, melted
1 tablespoon Chive Oil (page 51)

Heat the oven to 450 degrees. Adjust the oven rack to the lowest position.

Combine Roquefort, Boursin and 1 tablespoon butter in a food processor or blender and process until smooth. Transfer to a bowl and fold in Cognac, whipped cream, chives and salt and pepper. Mix thoroughly. Set aside at room temperature.

Stack the 3 sheets of phyllo on a nonstick baking sheet. Lightly brush the top sheet with melted butter. Bake until golden brown, 5 to 7 minutes. Let cool.

Cut a 2 × 8-inch strip from the phyllo and set aside. Spread or pipe the cheese mixture evenly over the large phyllo sheet. Refrigerate until firm, about 1 hour. When firm, cut into three 2 × 8-inch strips. Stack the strips

Millefeuille of Roquefort and Boursin

one on top of the other. Top with the reserved strip. Warm in the oven for 30 seconds. Cut into serving pieces. Serve with a sprinkling of Chive Oil.

SERVES 4

■

TRUFFLED BRIE

2 one-pound rounds ripe brie
1 pound mascarpone or sour cream
2 medium truffles, finely chopped
¼ cup truffle juice*

Trim off and discard the top rind from each round of brie. Combine the remaining ingredients and spread the mixture smoothly over the cut surface of one round. Cover with the other round, cut surface down. Cover tightly and refrigerate overnight. Bring to room temperature (about ½ hour) before serving.

SERVES 12

*Truffle juice can be purchased in cans. You may also use the liquid in which jarred or canned truffles are packed.

Substitute a duxelle of fresh mushrooms for the truffle and truffle juice, if you prefer.

Mushroom Duxelles: Mince ½ pound of button mushrooms, shiitake mushrooms or morels. Sauté in ¼ cup extra virgin olive oil over medium-high heat until all but ½ cup of their liquid has evaporated. Add 2 tablespoons chopped chives and let cool. When cool, stir in the mascarpone.

CHEESE GALETTE WITH PECANS

5 ounces Port-Salut, at room temperature
⅓ cup Roquefort, at room temperature
5 tablespoons sweet butter
1 egg, beaten
1 cup pecans, finely chopped, plus 4 whole
*   pecans for garnish*

Combine the cheeses and 3 tablespoons butter in a food processor or blender. Process until smooth. Shape into 4 patties, about ¾ inch thick. Dip into beaten egg and then into chopped pecans to coat. Melt 2 tablespoons butter in a medium sauté pan over medium-high heat. Add the patties and cook until golden brown, about 1½ minutes per side. Garnish with whole pecans.

SERVES 4

BROCCOLI MOUSSE WITH TRUFFLE VINAIGRETTE

This melt-in-your-mouth mousse can be served as a starter or side dish.

1 pound broccoli, trimmed and cut into
*   chunks*
¼ teaspoon unflavored gelatin
¼ cup heavy cream, whipped
Salt and freshly ground pepper to taste
2 tablespoons Truffle Vinaigrette (page 22),
*   Peanut Vinaigrette (page 21), or*
*   Hazelnut Vinaigrette (page 20)*

Cook the broccoli in boiling salted water until tender, 6 to 8 minutes. Drain and place in a food processor or blender. Process to a smooth purée. Sprinkle gelatin over the purée and process for 5 seconds. Transfer to a bowl and fold in the whipped cream thoroughly. Season with salt and pepper.

Pour into 4 well-buttered 3- or 4-ounce ramekins. Cover tightly and refrigerate until set, about 2 hours. Unmold by running a sharp knife around the inside rim. Serve with the Truffle Vinaigrette.

SERVES 4

WILD MUSHROOM GATEAU

If the varieties of mushrooms called for are not available, just use as many different varieties as you can find. The greater the variety of mushrooms, the more distinctive the flavor will be.

> *Crêpes (below)*
> *Mushroom Duxelles (right)*
> *1 cup Hazelnut Vinaigrette (page 20)*

Heat the oven to 400 degrees. Divide the Mushroom Duxelles among 7 of the Crêpes and spread evenly over each, right to the edges. Neatly stack the filled crêpes and place the plain crêpe on the top. Transfer to a baking sheet and warm in the oven for about 10 minutes. Serve with Hazelnut Vinaigrette.

SERVES 8

CREPES

> *¼ cup sweet butter*
> *1 cup all-purpose flour*
> *3 eggs*
> *1 cup milk*
> *Pinch salt*

Melt the butter in a small saucepan and cook until golden brown. Let cool until just warm.

Put the flour in a large mixing bowl. Add the eggs, milk and salt. Whisk well until batter is smooth and has no lumps. Whisk in the butter thoroughly. Cover the batter and let it rest in the refrigerator for 20 minutes.

Heat a 4- to 5-inch nonstick pan over medium-high heat. When hot, pour in just enough batter to cover the bottom of the pan. Cook until golden, then turn over to cook the other side (cook about 30 seconds per side). Repeat until you have 8 crêpes. Stack crêpes as they are made.

MAKES 8 CREPES

MUSHROOM DUXELLES

> *1 cup chanterelle mushrooms*
> *1 cup black trumpet mushrooms*
> *1 cup button mushrooms*
> *1 cup shiitake mushrooms*
> *1 tablespoon sweet butter*
> *1 clove garlic, peeled and chopped*
> *1 shallot, peeled and chopped*
> *Salt and freshly ground pepper to taste*
> *1 tablespoon chopped chervil*
> *1 tablespoon chopped chives*

Wash and finely chop the mushrooms. Melt the butter in a medium sauté pan over medium-high heat. Add the garlic and shallot and cook until translucent. Add the mushrooms, salt and pepper. Reduce heat to medium and cook until the mushroom liquid evaporates. Transfer to a medium mixing bowl. Stir in the chervil and chives.

SWISS CHARD TIMBALES

Swiss chard has a pronounced flavor that is superb with roast meats and chicken.

1 pound Swiss chard, washed thoroughly
and tough stems discarded
1 cup water
2 tablespoons fresh lemon juice
2 cloves garlic, peeled and chopped
2 cups heavy cream
2 tablespoons freshly grated Parmesan
1 egg yolk
Salt, freshly ground pepper and freshly
ground nutmeg to taste

Cut the white part of Swiss chard into small dice. Reserve the greens.

In a large pot, bring the water to a boil with lemon juice and a pinch of salt. Add the diced Swiss chard and simmer until tender, about 10 minutes. Drain and set aside. Blanch the greens in boiling salted water until soft, less than 1 minute. Drain and set aside.

In a medium saucepan, combine the garlic and the cream. Reduce over medium heat by three-fourths. Add Parmesan, egg yolk, salt, pepper and nutmeg. Add diced Swiss chard and mix well.

Line 4 espresso-size cups or 2-ounce ramekins with plastic wrap. Line the plastic completely with the greens, leaving an overhang around the top. Fill cups with the cream mixture and fold the greens over the top. Cover tightly with plastic wrap. Steam for 15 minutes. Unmold and serve.

SERVES 4

BOUILLON WITH BASIL DUMPLINGS

This is my version of a Provençal *soupe au pistou*, a vegetable soup with a garnish of basil-scented purée.

>   2 tablespoons extra virgin olive oil
>   1 medium carrot, peeled and diced
>   1 medium onion, peeled and diced
>   1 medium leek, washed thoroughly and
>   diced
>   1 stalk celery, diced
>   1 medium Idaho potato, peeled and diced
>   Salt to taste
>   6 cups water
>   1 Bouquet Garni (page 194)
>   ½ cup fresh or frozen peas
>   12 string beans
>   Potato and Basil Purée (page 150)
>
>   Garnish: 4 large basil leaves

In a large pot, heat the olive oil over medium-high heat. When hot, add the diced vegetables. Season with salt, cover the pot and let the vegetables cook for 5 minutes. Add water and Bouquet Garni. Let simmer for ½ hour. Add peas and string beans and simmer 10 minutes longer. Discard Bouquet Garni.

Shape dumplings by molding spoonfuls of Potato and Basil Purée using 2 tablespoons or soup spoons into oval shapes. Put 3 dumplings into each of 4 soup plates. Bring the broth to a boil. Ladle broth over the dumplings, garnish with basil leaves and serve immediately.

SERVES 4

TOMATO CONSOMME WITH PEA PANCAKES

A true consommé is made from meat or poultry broth. This vegetable broth is easily made sparkling clear by a classic technique. The eggshells and beaten whites absorb any impurities in the broth. If you like, put a pea pancake in each soup plate before filling with consommé—but serve right away so it doesn't get soggy.

> 2 pounds tomatoes, quartered
> 2 cups tomato juice
> 1 stalk celery with leaves, chopped
> 1 cup (lightly packed) basil leaves and stems
> 5 egg whites, shells reserved
> Salt to taste
> 3 drops tabasco
>
> Garnish: 1 tomato, peeled, seeded and
>   diced
>   4 large basil leaves, cut into ribbons
>   Pea Pancakes (right)

Combine tomatoes and tomato juice in a food processor or blender. Process until almost completely smooth. Pour mixture into a large pot and add the celery, basil leaves and stems and the eggshells. Bring to a boil over medium-high heat. Reduce heat to medium and simmer for 10 minutes.

Whisk the egg whites lightly. Remove the tomato mixture from the heat and slowly whisk in the egg whites. Reduce heat to medium-low and add salt and tabasco. Simmer for 10 minutes longer. Strain through a double layer of cheesecloth.

Serve the consommé either hot or cold and garnish with diced tomato and basil ribbons. Serve Pea Pancakes on the side.

SERVES 4

PEA PANCAKES

> ½ pound fresh or frozen peas (1½ cups)
> 1 whole egg plus 1 egg yolk
> Scant ½ cup heavy cream
> 3 tablespoons all-purpose flour
> 5 tablespoons sweet butter
> Salt and freshly ground pepper to taste

Cook the peas in boiling salted water until tender. Drain and set aside. Combine the peas, egg, yolk, cream and flour in a food processor or blender and process until smooth. Brown 3 tablespoons butter and add to the egg mixture. Process to combine thoroughly and season with salt and pepper. Set aside until ready to use.

Melt the remaining 2 tablespoons butter in a medium sauté pan. Use about 1 tablespoon batter for each pancake. Cook on both sides until golden brown around the edges.

Tomato Consommé with Pea Pancakes

OATMEAL PANCAKES

Serve these pancakes with applesauce or cranberry sauce and crisp bacon for breakfast. They are exquisite as an accompaniment to any fish. Try them with crème fraîche and smoked fish or caviar.

Scant ½ cup milk
1⅓ cups quick-cooking oats
1 egg
1 tablespoon chopped parsley
1 tablespoon chopped cilantro
Salt and freshly ground pepper to taste
¼ cup sweet butter
3 tablespoons chopped shallots (2 medium shallots)
3 tablespoons chopped onion

Bring the milk to a boil and pour it over the oats. Let rest for 10 minutes. Stir in the egg, parsley, cilantro, salt and pepper.

Melt 2 tablespoons butter in a small sauté pan over medium-high heat. Add the shallots and onion and cook until translucent. Add to the oatmeal batter.

Melt the remaining 2 tablespoons butter in a skillet. When hot, add the batter, 1 tablespoon per pancake. Cook until golden brown on both sides, about 30 seconds per side.

SERVES 4

SKEWERED POLENTA

Scant 1 cup milk
⅔ cup yellow cornmeal (stoneground if possible)
1 egg yolk
2 tablespoons freshly grated Parmesan cheese
Honey-Ginger Glazed Shallots (page 141)

In a medium saucepan, bring the milk to a boil over medium-high heat. Slowly add the cornmeal and cook for 10 minutes, stirring constantly. Remove from heat and add the egg yolk and cheese. Pour into a loaf pan, 9 × 5 × 3 inches. Cover tightly and refrigerate until firm, about 10 minutes.

Cut into 1-inch cubes and thread 4 cubes onto each of 6 skewers. Grill until lightly marked or sauté in 2 tablespoons olive oil until golden brown. Serve with Honey-Ginger Glazed Shallots.

SERVES 6

CORN MUFFINS

½ cup fresh or frozen corn
½ cup yellow cornmeal (stoneground if
    possible)
½ tablespoon baking powder
½ teaspoon baking soda
½ teaspoon sugar
½ teaspoon salt
¼ cup all-purpose flour
2 tablespoons melted sweet butter
¼ cup heavy cream
½ cup buttermilk
1 egg, separated

Heat the oven to 400 degrees.

Combine the corn and cornmeal in a food processor or blender and process for 30 seconds.

In a large mixing bowl, combine the dry ingredients. Add the corn mixture.

Combine the butter, cream, buttermilk and egg yolk and mix thoroughly. Add to the dry ingredients. Beat until smooth.

Beat the egg white to stiff peaks. Fold into the batter.

Butter 6 cups of a regular-size muffin tin. Pour batter into each cup to fill three-fourths. Bake for 15 minutes.

MAKES 6 MUFFINS

CORN PANCAKES

Two pancakes make an ample side dish serving to accompany roast duck, goose, turkey or any bird.

⅔ cup yellow cornmeal (stoneground if
    possible)
Scant 1 cup all-purpose flour
Pinch sugar
2 eggs
1 cup milk
¾ cup fresh or frozen corn
2 tablespoons sweet butter

In a large mixing bowl, combine the dry ingredients. Add eggs, milk, corn and 1½ tablespoons butter, melted and cooked until golden brown. Mix well.

Melt the remaining ½ tablespoon butter in a medium sauté pan. Use about 1 tablespoon batter for each pancake. Cook until golden brown on both sides, 30 seconds per side.

SERVES 10

SPICED RICE

These cakes have a light crust but the rice inside is moist. This is a perfect complement to the soft shell crabs on page 65 and many of the Oriental dishes. I like to use basmati rice for this dish; the thin grains have extraordinary fragrance.

> 1 cup long-grain rice
> 2½ cups water
> 1 stick cinnamon
> 1 bay leaf, broken into large pieces
> 3 cloves
> 5 black peppercorns
> Pinch salt
> 2 tablespoons Clarified Butter (page 194)
>   or sweet butter
> Large pinch saffron threads

In a medium saucepan, combine the rice, water, cinnamon, bay leaf, cloves, peppercorns and salt. Cook over high heat for 10 minutes, until most of the water is absorbed.

Turn the rice into a strainer and rinse well under cold running water to remove excess starch. Discard the cinnamon and bay leaf pieces.

Heat the oven to 450 degrees.

Lightly butter the bottoms of four 3- to 4-ounce nonstick molds or one 8-inch nonstick pan. Scatter a few saffron threads over the bottom of the molds.

Pack rice into the molds no more than ½ to ¾ inch deep.

Bake for 10 minutes. Unmold carefully. If a single large mold is used, cut into portions.

SERVES 4

■

RICE CRACKERS

Savory and incredibly thin—these crackers are habit-forming and very easy to make.

> 1 cup cooked risotto (page 163)

Heat the oven to 450 degrees.

Spread the risotto on nonstick baking sheets in a paper-thin layer. Bake until pale gold, about 5 minutes. Remove from the oven and cut into crackers, using a pizza wheel or sharp knife. Return to the oven and bake until golden brown and crisp, 3 to 5 minutes longer. Serve hot or cold.

SERVES 4

CRISPS OF RISOTTO

We overcook the risotto for these crisps so the individual grains of rice seem to "melt" together.

> ¼ cup sweet butter
> 2 medium shallots, peeled and chopped
> (about 3 tablespoons)
> ½ cup Arborio rice
> 3 cups Mixed Vegetable Broth (page 75)
> ¼ cup freshly grated Parmesan
> Salt and freshly ground pepper to taste

Heat the oven to 450 degrees. Melt 2 tablespoons butter in an oven-proof pan over medium-high heat. Add the shallots and cook until translucent, about 1 minute.

Add the rice and sauté for 2 minutes, stirring constantly. Add the Mixed Vegetable Broth, cheese, salt and pepper. Cover and bake for 20 minutes.

Remove from oven and spread mixture evenly in a jelly roll pan. Cover and refrigerate for 1 hour.

Shape into patties about 2 inches across and ½ inch thick. Melt the remaining 2 tablespoons butter in a large sauté pan over medium-high heat. When hot, add patties and cook until crisp and golden brown on both sides, about 2 minutes.

MAKES 12 CRISPS

ONION JAM

Serve this rich jam with hot buttered toast, red meat or boiled potatoes. It will keep, tightly covered and refrigerated, for months.

> 5 tablespoons sweet butter
> 1½ pounds onions, peeled and thinly sliced
> ¾ cup sugar
> ½ cup grenadine
> ½ cup red wine
> ½ cup red wine vinegar

Melt the butter in a large sauté pan over medium-high heat. Add the onions and cook until translucent, about 4 minutes, stirring occasionally. Add remaining ingredients and reduce heat to low. Cook for 1½ hours, stirring occasionally, until all liquid has evaporated.

SERVES 12

FRUITS, SORBETS, ICE CREAMS AND SWEETS

■

The desserts that follow were created in a spirit of lightness and simplicity. They contain no flour, and many are made without eggs. At Restaurant Lafayette we found traditional baked desserts were just too heavy after several courses. And, the idea of rapidly made desserts, refreshing and luscious with the flavors and textures of seasonal fruit, appealed to me as the perfect final note.

I'm including, too, a variety of rather different ice creams, sorbets and granités (simple ices) that are wonderful on their own and especially nice served with the fruit desserts. Granités are very nice when served between courses, too. They can provide a refreshing break in the middle of longer menus, or when courses change from seafood to meat. They are so light that you can use them as you like.

Back to front: Apricot Gratin with Almond Milk Ice Cream (page 168), Hot Cherries with Honey Kirsch (page 171) on Pistachio Ice Cream (page 172), Sautéed Rhubarb with Strawberries (page 166).

SAUTEED RHUBARB WITH STRAWBERRIES

2 tablespoons sweet butter
4 cups peeled rhubarb, cut into ½-inch
    chunks
2 tablespoons sugar
18 large strawberries
Vanilla ice cream
Vanilla Syrup (below)

Melt the butter in a large sauté pan over medium-high heat. Add the rhubarb, sprinkle with sugar and sauté until tender, 4 to 5 minutes. Mash 12 strawberries and slice the remaining 6 in half. Arrange rhubarb in the center of each of 4 dessert plates. Add a scoop of vanilla ice cream, crushed berries and top with sliced strawberries. Pour a little Vanilla Syrup around the outside of the plate.

SERVES 4

VANILLA SYRUP

½ large, moist vanilla bean
¼ cup Simple Syrup (page 195)

Slice the vanilla bean in half lengthwise. Scrape the vanilla grains into a small cup and mix with Simple Syrup. Reserve the bean for another use.

TROPICAL MEDLEY

1 tablespoon sweet butter
½ medium pineapple, peeled and cut into
    large dice
1 medium mango, peeled and cut into large
    dice
1 medium red papaya, peeled, seeded and
    cut into large dice
½ cup packed dark brown sugar
¾ cup dark rum
1 medium passion fruit
Lemon Grass Sorbet (page 176)

Melt the butter in a medium sauté pan over medium-high heat. Add pineapple and sauté for 1 minute. Add the mango and the papaya and sauté until hot. Cut the passion fruit in half and scrape the pulp and seeds into the pan. Sprinkle with sugar and deglaze the pan with the rum. Simmer for 2 minutes over medium heat to reduce liquid slightly. Transfer to a large plate and refrigerate until fruit has cooled to room temperature. To serve, spoon ½ cup of fruit onto each serving plate. Serve with Lemon Grass Sorbet.

SERVES 4

ORANGE BLOSSOM POTS DE CREME

1 quart plus 1 cup heavy cream
2 tablespoons orange blossom (orange
    flower) water
12 egg yolks
½ cup sugar

Garnish: Rose Petal Jam (right)
              2 tablespoons chopped pistachios

Heat the oven to 250 degrees.

In a large saucepan, combine the cream and orange blossom water over medium-high heat. Bring to a boil and immediately remove from heat. Let sit at room temperature for ½ hour. Whisk egg yolks and sugar together until light and fluffy. Bring the cream mixture back to a boil and pour in a thin stream into the yolks, whisking constantly. Strain the mixture and ladle into eight 3- to 4-ounce ramekins. Place ramekins in a deep baking pan. Pour hot water into the pan to reach halfway up the ramekins. Bake for 30 to 40 minutes, until a knife inserted in the center comes out clean. Let cool to room temperature. Cover tightly and refrigerate for 2 hours before serving. Garnish each pot de crème with a dollop of Rose Petal Jam and a sprinkling of pistachios.

SERVES 8

ROSE PETAL JAM

½ cup Simple Syrup (page 195)
1 cup pink rose petals (unsprayed)
1 tablespoon rose water
1 teaspoon fresh lemon juice

In a small saucepan, bring the Simple Syrup to a simmer over low heat. Add the rose petals, rose water and lemon juice. Cook, stirring occasionally, until the petals are wilted and syrup is thick, about 10 minutes.

COLD KIWI SOUP

When a food mill is used to purée the kiwis, the resulting color is a brilliant green. A food processor or blender can be used, but it will liquify the fruit to a more pastel purée.

Scant 1 cup dry white wine
3 tablespoons honey
11 kiwis
1 medium apple (Cortland, Granny Smith or other tart apple)
2 tablespoons fresh lemon juice
¼ cup sugar
20 large strawberries, sliced in half

In a nonreactive saucepan, combine the wine and honey over medium-high heat. Bring to a boil, remove from heat and let cool to room temperature. Peel 8 kiwis, quarter them and remove the white pith. Put through the medium disc of a food mill and mix the purée with the wine syrup. Cover tightly and refrigerate at least 3 hours.

Peel remaining kiwis and cut into eighths. Peel and dice the apple. Toss first in the lemon juice, then sugar. Arrange kiwi and strawberry slices around the inside of each of 4 soup plates. Ladle in cold kiwi mixture over the fruit and garnish with a few pieces of sugared apple.

SERVES 4

APRICOT GRATIN WITH ALMOND MILK ICE CREAM

1 cup finely ground almonds
2 tablespoons plus 4 teaspoons sweet butter
4 teaspoons sugar
4 teaspoons amaretto
8 apricots, halved and pitted
¼ cup dry white wine
Almond Milk Ice Cream (page 172)

Heat the oven to 450 degrees.

Mix the ground almonds, 4 teaspoons butter, sugar and amaretto to a paste. Fill the apricot halves with the mixture.

Place the stuffed apricots in a broiler-proof pan. Pour the wine around them and add the remaining 2 tablespoons butter. Bake for 10 minutes. Remove from the oven and place under a preheated broiler, about 6 inches from the heat, to glaze the almond filling. Remove apricots to serving plates. Reduce the cooking liquid to a syrup. Serve the apricots with Almond Milk Ice Cream and some of the syrup.

SERVES 4

LITCHIS WITH BITTER ALMOND PANCAKES

Fresh litchis are admittedly a luxury. If they are not to be found, substitute canned litchis; they will not need to be cooked.

> 24 fresh litchis, peeled and rinsed
> 1 cup sugar
> 4 cups water
> 2 tablespoons fresh lemon juice
> Bitter Almond Pancakes (right)

In a large saucepan, combine the litchis, sugar, water and lemon juice over medium heat. Poach the litchis until they are tender, about 10 minutes.

Let cool in the poaching liquid. When cooled to room temperature, cover tightly and refrigerate until cold.

Serve 6 litchis per person with some of the poaching liquid and Bitter Almond Pancakes on the side.

SERVES 4

BITTER ALMOND PANCAKES

> 1 cup finely ground almonds
> 1 egg
> 1 egg yolk
> ¾ cup heavy cream
> 1 tablespoon sugar
> 4 tablespoons sweet butter, cooked until golden brown and cooled
> 2 tablespoons almond extract

Heat the oven to 350 degrees.

Mix all ingredients to a smooth batter. Spoon onto a nonstick baking sheet, using 1 teaspoon batter for each pancake. Bake for 10 minutes. Turn the pancakes over and bake for 2 minutes longer. Let cool slightly on the baking sheet.

WINTER COMPOTE

*Scant ½ cup each of the following unsweet-
  ened, dried fruits*: raisins, currants, cherries, blueberries, cranberries, strawberries,
  dates, pears, peaches, figs and apricots*
Grated zest of 1 medium orange
2 tablespoons sugar
1 tablespoon honey
2 tablespoons chopped fresh ginger
*1 moist vanilla bean, halved lengthwise and
  the grains loosened*
1 stick cinnamon
1 tablespoon fresh lemon juice
2 cups dry red wine
Bitter Cocoa Sorbet (page 177)

Cut the larger dried fruits into strips; keep
small ones whole.

In a medium nonreactive saucepan, combine
the remaining ingredients except the sorbet
over medium-high heat. Bring to a boil, add
the fruits and simmer for 20 minutes. Remove
vanilla bean and cinnamon stick. Serve with
Bitter Cocoa Sorbet.

SERVES 4

*Use as great a variety of dried fruits as you
can find—the more, the better.

APPLE COMPOTE WITH ROSEMARY

4 medium Granny Smith apples
¾ cup sliced almonds
1 tablespoon sweet butter
2 tablespoons plus 2 teaspoons honey
*¼ teaspoon fresh rosemary leaves or ⅛ tea-
  spoon dried rosemary*
½ cup plus 2 tablespoons water
4 apricots, peeled and pitted
2 tablespoons Simple Syrup (page 195)

Peel the apples and cut into small dice. Put in
a medium saucepan with the almonds, butter, honey, rosemary and ½ cup water. Cover
and cook over medium-low heat until liquid
evaporates. Uncover and cook until apples
caramelize, about 5 minutes longer. Add ½
cup water and cook until it evaporates. Set
aside and keep warm.

Combine the apricots, 2 tablespoons water
and Simple Syrup in a blender. Blend until
smooth. Serve with the compote.

SERVES 4

ROAST FIGS WITH PORT WINE

16 medium figs
2 teaspoons sweet butter
¾ cup Port wine
¾ cup dry red wine
1 stick cinnamon
1 teaspoon fresh lemon juice
Three-Spice Ice Cream (page 173)

Heat the oven to 450 degrees.

Slash each fig 2 or 3 times. Melt the butter in an ovenproof pan over medium-high heat and add the figs. Cook for 1 minute. Deglaze the pan with Port and red wine and add cinnamon stick. Put the pan in the oven and roast for 5 minutes.

Remove the figs. Reduce the cooking liquid on top of the stove to a syrup and add the lemon juice. Arrange the figs in small bowls around scoops of Three-Spice Ice Cream with some of the sauce spooned on top.

SERVES 4

HOT CHERRIES WITH HONEY KIRSCH

4 teaspoons honey
4 cups pitted fresh sweet cherries
2 teaspoons sweet butter
2 teaspoons kirsch
Pistachio Ice Cream (page 172)

Garnish: 4 teaspoons chopped pistachios

In a medium sauté pan, cook the honey over medium-high heat until it caramelizes, about 2 minutes. Add the cherries and stir to coat well. Add the butter and stir until it melts. Deglaze the pan with kirsch and cook for 2 minutes longer.

Put a scoop of Pistachio Ice Cream in each of 4 serving dishes. Pour the cherries and sauce over the ice cream and sprinkle with chopped pistachios.

SERVES 4

ALMOND MILK ICE CREAM

2 cups milk
2 cups heavy cream
1 moist vanilla bean
8 egg whites
⅔ cup sugar
1 cup finely ground almonds

Combine milk and cream. Cut the vanilla bean in half lengthwise and, with the point of a knife, scrape the tiny seeds into the cream mixture. Add the bean and let infuse for ½ hour.

In a mixing bowl, combine the egg whites and sugar. Bring the cream mixture to a boil. Slowly pour about one-third of the cream mixture over the egg whites and sugar, whisking vigorously. Pour the mixture into the saucepan, bring to a boil, and boil for 1 minute, stirring constantly with a wooden spoon. Pour the mixture into a mixing bowl and stir in the ground almonds. Let cool to room temperature, then strain. Process in an ice cream maker according to the manufacturer's instructions.

MAKES ABOUT 6 CUPS

PISTACHIO ICE CREAM

1½ cups milk
1½ cups heavy cream
1½ cups pistachios
8 egg yolks
½ cup sugar

In a medium saucepan, combine the milk, cream and pistachios. Bring to a boil, remove from the heat and let infuse for 1 hour.

Pour the mixture into a food processor or blender. Process until nuts are finely chopped; return the mixture to the saucepan. Whisk the egg yolks and sugar until light and fluffy. Bring the pistachio cream to a boil. Pour about one-third of the pistachio cream over the yolks while beating vigorously. Pour the mixture back into the saucepan. Cook over very low heat, stirring constantly with a wooden spoon, until thick enough to coat the spoon. Remove from heat and strain into a medium mixing bowl. Set the bowl into a larger bowl of ice water and whisk until cool. (Or cover and refrigerate until cool.) Process in an ice cream maker according to the manufacturer's instructions.

MAKES ABOUT 5 CUPS

GINGER ICE CREAM

1 cup coarsely chopped plus 2 table-
spoons finely chopped fresh ginger
1½ cups milk
1½ cups heavy cream
8 egg yolks
½ cup sugar

Put the coarsely chopped ginger in a small saucepan with just enough water to cover. Boil for 5 minutes. Drain the ginger and put it in a medium saucepan with the milk and cream. Bring to a boil; let infuse for 1 hour.

Whisk the yolks and sugar until light and fluffy. Bring the ginger cream to a boil. Pour about one-third of the ginger cream over the yolks while beating vigorously. Pour the mixture back into the saucepan. Cook over very low heat, stirring constantly with a wooden spoon, until thick enough to coat the spoon. Remove from heat and strain into a medium mixing bowl. Set the bowl into a larger bowl of ice water. (Or cover and refrigerate until cool.) Add finely chopped ginger and process in an ice cream maker according to the manufacturer's intructions.

MAKES ABOUT 5 CUPS

THREE-SPICE ICE CREAM

1½ cups milk
1½ cups heavy cream
¼ cup crushed star anise or fennel seed
3 sticks cinnamon
2 teaspoons ground allspice
8 egg yolks
½ cup sugar
½ teaspoon finely chopped fresh ginger

In a medium saucepan, combine the milk, cream and spices. Bring to a boil and let infuse for 1 hour.

Strain into a clean saucepan. Whisk the yolks and sugar until light and fluffy. Bring the spice cream to a boil. Pour about one-third of the spice cream over the yolks while beating vigorously. Pour the mixture back into the saucepan. Cook over very low heat, stirring constantly with a wooden spoon, until thick enough to coat the spoon. Remove from heat and strain into a medium mixing bowl. Set the bowl into a larger bowl of ice water. (Or cover and refrigerate until cool.) Add finely chopped ginger and process in an ice cream maker according to the manufacturer's instructions.

MAKES ABOUT 5 CUPS

Following Pages, from left to right: Cranberry-Champagne Granité (page 178), Bitter Cocoa Sorbet (page 177), Grapefruit-Campari Granité (page 178), Orange-Lillet Granité (page 179), Tamarillo Sorbet (page 177), Lemon Grass Sorbet (page 176).

CARDAMOM ICE CREAM

1½ cups milk
1½ cups heavy cream
2 tablespoons crushed green cardamom
* seeds*
Grated zest of 1 small orange
8 egg yolks
½ cup sugar

In a medium saucepan, combine the milk, cream, cardamom seeds and orange zest. Bring to a boil and let infuse for 1 hour.

Strain into a clean saucepan. Whisk the yolks and sugar until light and fluffy. Bring the cream mixture to a boil. Pour about one-third of the cream mixture over the yolks while beating vigorously. Pour the mixture back into the saucepan. Cook over very low heat, stirring constantly with a wooden spoon, until thick enough to coat the spoon. Remove from heat and strain into a medium mixing bowl. Set the bowl into a larger bowl of ice water. (Or cover and refrigerate until cool.) Process in an ice cream maker according to the manufacturer's instructions.

MAKES ABOUT 4½ CUPS

LEMON GRASS SORBET

2 cups fresh lemon juice
2 cups dry white wine
½ cup light corn syrup
⅔ cup sugar
7 stalks lemon grass, coarsely chopped

In a medium nonreactive saucepan, combine all ingredients. Bring to a boil and let infuse for 1 hour. Strain the liquid and process in an ice cream maker according to manufacturer's instructions.

MAKES ABOUT 5 CUPS

BITTER COCOA SORBET

1¾ cups water
½ cup sugar
Grated zest of 1 medium orange
½ cup good-quality cocoa powder
3½ ounces good-quality unsweetened
    chocolate, melted

In a medium saucepan, combine the water, sugar and zest. Bring to a boil and whisk in the cocoa powder and chocolate. When the mixture returns to a boil, remove from heat and strain into a medium mixing bowl. Set the bowl into a larger bowl of ice water. (Or cover and refrigerate until cool.) Process in an ice cream maker according to the manufacturer's instructions.

MAKES ABOUT 3½ CUPS

TAMARILLO SORBET

9 tamarillos, peeled and coarsely chopped
1¾ cups sugar
3 cups dry white wine

In a medium nonreactive saucepan, combine all ingredients. Bring to a boil and simmer for 4 minutes. Transfer to a food processor or blender and process until smooth. Strain and let cool. Process in an ice cream maker according to the manufacturer's instructions.

MAKES ABOUT 5 CUPS

A WORD ABOUT GRANITES

Granités are made differently than sorbets. Where a sorbet is smooth, a proper granité is made up of larger icy particles. Depending on the composition of a particular granité (and how it is scraped from its freezing tray), a granité can be served as an icy mound of delicate flakes or chunky grains.

CRANBERRY-CHAMPAGNE GRANITE

1 cup cranberry juice
2 tablespoons Simple Syrup (page 195)
1 cup brut Champagne

Combine all ingredients. Pour into a 13 × 9-inch baking pan and freeze for 4 hours.

Remove from the freezer. Scrape the surface of the ice with a spoon or fork into large flaky crystals.

MAKES ABOUT 2 CUPS

GRAPEFRUIT-CAMPARI GRANITE

2 cups fresh grapefruit juice
¼ cup Simple Syrup (page 195)
2 tablespoons Campari

Combine all ingredients. Pour into a 13 × 9-inch baking pan and freeze for 4 hours.

Remove from the freezer. Scrape the surface of the ice with a spoon or fork into large flaky crystals.

MAKES ABOUT 2¼ CUPS

■

TEQUILA-LIME GRANITE

1¼ cups fresh lime juice
¼ cup water
¼ cup Simple Syrup (page 195)
½ cup tequila

Combine all ingredients. Pour into a 13 × 9-inch baking pan and freeze for 4 hours.

Remove from the freezer. Scrape the surface of the ice with a spoon or fork into large flaky crystals.

MAKES ABOUT 2¼ CUPS

ORANGE-LILLET GRANITE

2 cups fresh orange juice
¼ cup Simple Syrup (page 195)
½ cup light Lillet

Combine all ingredients. Pour into a 13 × 9-inch baking pan and freeze for 4 hours.

Remove from the freezer. Scrape the surface of the ice with a spoon or fork into large flaky crystals.

MAKES ABOUT 2 ¾ CUPS

ESPRESSO-LEMON GRANITE

1¼ cups decaffeinated espresso
¼ cup Tia Maria or similar coffee-flavored liqueur
¼ cup Simple Syrup (page 195)
¾ cup water
1 tablespoon grated lemon zest

Combine all ingredients. Pour into a 13 × 9-inch baking pan and freeze for 4 hours.

Remove from the freezer. Scrape the surface of the ice with a spoon or fork into large flaky crystals.

MAKES ABOUT 2 ½ CUPS

AN AMERICAN ACCENT

■

You can see from the recipes that follow that I've been experimenting a bit with American cooking. I really like American food, sometimes crave it.

Lots of us prefer straightforward, simply flavored food. It has been my experience that even those who are dubious about "fancy" food (including children who turn up their noses at most "grown-up" food) positively devour the Tuna Sandwich (page 182) and the Lamb Burger (page 186). The Shrimp Cocktail (page 182) is unbelievably easy for all its unusual effect—perfect for entertaining—and the Tomato Salad (page 187) is for anyone who ever felt they couldn't get too much of a good thing.

Americans excel at many things, and one of these is barbecue. I wouldn't presume to tell an American how to barbecue, but I'd like to suggest that flavored oils make exceptional marinades. Marinate the foods that follow in the suggested oils, for starters, but feel free to try other flavored oils, too. Simply prepare the oil of your choice. Marinate the meat or seafood in the refrigerator overnight (or at least 6 hours) in enough oil to half cover it. Turn it several times if possible while it marinates.

RIBS	Paprika Oil
STEAK	all Mild Herb Oils, Garlic, Mustard and Rosemary Oil
HAMBURGER	all Mild Herb Oils, Cumin and Wasabi Oil
CHICKEN	Curry, Ginger, Orange-Basil and Tarragon Oil
FISH	all Herb Oils, Fennel, Lobster, Saffron and Shrimp Oil
SHRIMP	Cardamom, Curry, Ginger, Lobster, Pineapple-Cilantro and Shrimp Oil

Marinating for barbecue, *clockwise from top:* scallops in Orange Oil, lamb in Basil Oil, veal in Paprika Oil, chicken in Curry Oil, shrimp in Shrimp Oil.

AMERICAN ICED SHRIMP COCKTAIL

*2 cups fresh (strained) or canned tomato
   juice*
Pinch celery salt
Dash tabasco
2 tablespoons prepared horseradish
Salt and freshly ground pepper to taste
1 pound jumbo shrimp, peeled and deveined
Small leaves of arugula or basil

Thoroughly combine all ingredients except shrimp and arugula. Pour into a flat container to a depth of ½ inch. Freeze until firm.

In a Chinese wok or steamer, steam the shrimp for 3 minutes (10 minutes for shrimp wrapped in plastic wrap, if following the technique on page 104). Let shrimp rest 1 minute. Divide the shrimp among 4 serving plates.

Break the tomato ice into pieces and arrange about ¼ cup next to the shrimp on each plate. Decorate with arugula leaves.

SERVES 4

TUNA SANDWICH

I love this sandwich cooked quickly, 1 minute per side. Use ordinary white bread as you would for any sandwich. You may want to try this with salmon instead of tuna.

*2 slices white sandwich bread, crusts
   trimmed*
3-ounce slice fresh tuna (1 inch thick)
1 egg yolk beaten with 1 tablespoon water
2 tablespoons extra virgin olive oil
Salt and freshly ground pepper to taste

With a rolling pin, flatten each slice of bread until thin.

Trim the tuna so it will fit neatly on one slice of bread, leaving a ¼-inch border around the tuna.

Brush one slice of bread, right to the edges, with egg yolk. Place the tuna in the center and season lightly with salt and pepper.

Cover with the other slice of bread. Press the edges together to make a package; the egg will help seal it.

In a small sauté pan, heat the olive oil until hot. Add the sandwich and cook over medium-high heat until golden brown on both sides, about 1 minute per side for rare tuna, 2 minutes per side for medium.

Remove from the pan and lightly pat dry with paper toweling to remove excess oil. Cut into quarters and serve immediately.

SERVES 1

POTATO CLUB SANDWICH

This "sandwich" is built using crisp fried potatoes in place of bread. You can, of course, use any combination of meats for this sandwich. You can play with another American favorite in similar fashion, layering scrambled eggs and bacon with potato lattices. Enjoy!

1 large Idaho potato, peeled
1 cup melted sweet butter or peanut oil
3 or 4 leaves of salad greens
2 thin slices tomato
Extra virgin olive oil
Balsamic vinegar
2 or 3 thin slices ham
2 or 3 thin slices turkey
3 or 4 thin slices avocado
Salt and freshly ground pepper to taste

Heat the oven to 450 degrees.

Slice the potato lengthwise, no more than 1/16 inch thick. Use a mandoline if you have one. You want very thin, oval slices. Cut each slice into 4 thin rectangles. (A large potato will yield about 40 rectangular strips).

Toss the strips in butter and drain any excess. Arrange 8 strips with space between them in a grid on a nonstick baking sheet. (It will look like a large tic-tac-toe pattern.) Make 4 potato grids.

Bake until golden brown, 10 to 15 minutes. Gently turn over and bake until brown, about 5 minutes longer. Lightly salt.

To assemble the sandwich, place 1 potato grid on a serving plate. Cover with a few lettuce leaves and tomato slices lightly coated with a little olive oil and vinegar. Top with a potato grid. Cover with ham and turkey and top with another potato grid. Top with the remaining lettuce, avocado and a final potato grid. Drizzle some olive oil and vinegar around the plate. Serve with a sprig of fresh herb through the top.

SERVES 1

Following Pages, left to right: Tomato Salad with Tomato Water (page 187), Lamb Burgers with Goat Cheese (page 186), Tuna Sandwiches, Potato Club Sandwiches, American Iced Shrimp Cocktail.

LAMB BURGER WITH GOAT CHEESE

I made this dish on the grill this summer, using goat. With freshly made shoestring potatoes, it was a great treat.

1½ pounds ground lamb or baby goat
Pinch cayenne pepper
2 pinches ground cinammon
Salt and freshly ground pepper to taste
2 tablespoons chopped cilantro
¼ cup soft white goat cheese, such as
    Montrachet
Sauce (right)

Combine the lamb, cayenne pepper, cinnamon, salt and pepper. Shape into 4 patties. Combine the cilantro and cheese. Make a pocket in the center of each patty and stuff with the cheese mixture. Cover the cheese completely with meat.

Sauté over medium-high heat or grill for 7 to 10 minutes (depending on how you like your burger cooked).

SERVES 4

SAUCE

1 cup plain goat or cow's milk yogurt
1 tablespoon cumin seeds
½ cup chopped, seeded cucumber
Pinch each salt and cayenne pepper

Combine all ingredients and refrigerate until needed.

TOMATO SALAD WITH TOMATO WATER

Tomato salad is a wonderful American dish. Remember that tomatoes are best in the summertime, and any tomato salad is only as good as the tomatoes that go into it.

Serve a little glass of the richly flavored Tomato Water with the salad, or with the Tomato and Basil Tart (page 112). To each cup of Tomato Water, add a few drops of vodka and tabasco sauce for a very light Bloody Mary.

4 ripe beefsteak or other large, flavorful tomatoes
Salt and freshly ground pepper to taste
¼ cup vinegar
½ cup extra virgin olive oil
1 tablespoon boiling water
1 teaspoon each chopped basil, mint and parsley

Blanch the tomatoes in boiling water for 30 seconds. Immediately refresh under cold running water for 10 seconds. Remove skins. Slice the tomatoes ½ inch thick and reserve the juice. Season tomatoes with salt and pepper.

Put the tomatoes and their juice in a bag made from 4 layers of cheesecloth. Suspend the bag over a large bowl in the refrigerator and allow "water" to drip for 4 hours. Keep Tomato Water refrigerated until ready to use.

Combine the vinegar, olive oil and boiling water in a blender. Blend until emulsified. Add basil, mint and parsley.

Arrange the tomato slices on a large serving plate and dress with vinaigrette.

SERVES 4, WITH 1½ TO 2 CUPS
TOMATO WATER

THIRTY-MINUTE MENUS AND MENUS FOR SPECIAL OCCASIONS

■

At the end of a busy day or even on the weekend, many of us don't want to bother cooking complicated meals that take a great deal of time to prepare. With only a little practice, the following menus may be prepared in less than 30 minutes.

When you have prepared any of the vinaigrettes, flavored oils or broths in advance, you'll save even more time. Remember, too, that you can make the fillings for the phyllo dishes in the morning or even a day ahead.

I haven't suggested desserts for these menus. Any of the ice creams, sorbets or granités would be very nice. In addition, the following desserts are very quick to prepare:

SAUTÉED RHUBARB WITH STRAWBERRIES   TROPICAL MEDLEY   COLD KIWI SOUP

APPLE COMPOTE WITH ROSEMARY

ROAST FIGS WITH PORT WINE   HOT CHERRIES WITH HONEY KIRSCH

The menus that follow are intended to help you put a marvelous dinner on the table with a minimum of time and fuss.

Of course you can combine any of the rapidly prepared appetizers with the sautéed or steamed dishes (pages 93 to 105) for an equally rapid meal. If I am preparing one course with a flavored oil, I like to use a broth, vinaigrette or juice in another course, because I enjoy the variety. You might prefer all-vinaigrette or all-juice menus, playing the flavors against each other.

Clockwise from top: Rare roast beef sandwiches with basil oil, Salmon Leaves with Rosemary Oil (page 108), Shrimp in Spicy Carrot Juice (page 11), Goat Cheese with Watercress Oil (page 151).

ASPARAGUS SALAD
MONKFISH WITH MUSHROOM SYRUP

■

COLD CUCUMBER SOUP WITH DILL OIL
LAMB IN A POTATO CRUST

■

SHRIMP SALAD WITH CURRY OIL
FILLET OF RED SNAPPER WITH CITRUS VINAIGRETTE

■

POACHED FOIE GRAS WITH FENNEL AND CARAMEL PEPPER
SALMON CABBAGE WITH JUNIPER VINAIGRETTE

■

VEAL IN RICE PAPER
WHITING WITH ENDIVE BROTH

■

TOMATO AND BASIL TART
SEA SCALLOPS WITH ZUCCHINI JUICE

■

FOIE GRAS WITH GINGER AND MANGO
SHRIMP WITH SPICY CARROT JUICE

■

RABBIT SAUSAGE WITH MUSTARD OIL
LOBSTER WITH ASPARAGUS JUICE

■

THAI SHRIMP CAKES
CHICKEN IN PINEAPPLE JUICE

■

ALSATIAN TART
HALIBUT WITH TRUFFLE AND YELLOW BELL PEPPER OIL

■

SHRIMP AND CHICKEN IN LEMON GRASS BROTH
RED SNAPPER WITH POTATO FLAKES AND TOMATO OIL

■

CHEESE GALLETTE WITH PECANS
COD CAKES WITH ORANGE-BASIL OIL

TEMPURA WITH CABBAGE SALAD AND CINNAMON OIL
WATERCRESS BROTH WITH YELLOW PIKE

■

SALMON LEAVES WITH ROSEMARY OIL
VEAL WITH CELERY JUICE AND ROQUEFORT

■

LOBSTER STRUDEL or SHRIMP, TOMATO AND
CILANTRO TART
LACQUERED QUAIL WITH SESAME SEEDS

■

CHANTERELLE AND SPINACH SALAD
CHICKEN WITH LIME AND HONEY

■

GOAT CHEESE WITH WATERCRESS OIL
TUNA SANDWICH

■

AMERICAN ICED SHRIMP COCKTAIL
LAMB BURGER WITH GOAT CHEESE

■

SHRIMP IN A SPICED ORANGE AND SAUTERNES BROTH
MARINATED LEMON CHICKEN WITH FENNEL OIL

■

GOAT CHEESE BRICKS WITH ENDIVE SALAD
WATERCRESS BROTH WITH YELLOW PIKE

■

RICE PAPER SUSHI
SOFT SHELL CRABS WITH CARROT-CINNAMON OIL

■

TUNA TARTARE WITH GAUFRETTE POTATOES
COD WITH PINK RADISH JUICE

■

TUNA TARTARE WITH ASSORTED CHIPS AND OILS
POTATO CLUB SANDWICH

MENUS FOR SPECIAL OCCASIONS

SPRING

Shrimp in Spicy Carrot Juice
Lamb in a Potato Crust
Sautéed Rhubarb with Strawberries

■

SUMMER

Sea Scallops with Zucchini Juice
Salmon in a Shiitake Shell
Cold Kiwi Soup

■

FALL

Alsatian Tart
Monkfish Medallions with Mushroom Syrup
Apple Compote with Rosemary

■

WINTER

Sweetbreads with Yellow Potato Salad
Halibut with Truffle and Yellow Bell Pepper Oil
Winter Compote with Bitter Cocoa Sorbet

MENU POISSONS

Tuna Tartare with Gaufrette Potatoes
Watercress Broth with Yellow Pike
Lobster with Parsnip Purée
Orange Blossom Pots de Crème

■

MENU DE FETES

Marble of Foie Gras
Sea Scallops in Leek "Juice"
Lamb in a Potato Crust
Hot Cherries with Honey Kirsch

■

MENU ORIENTAL

Eggs with Oyster
Thai Shrimp Cakes
Lacquered Quail with Sesame Seeds
Litchis with Bitter Almond Pancakes

PANTRY BASICS AND UNCOMMON GARNISHES

■

With these few basic ingredients on hand, you can be prepared for just about any recipe that appeals to you. I've come to think of the flavored oils, vinaigrettes, juices and broths as basics; at least, that is how I use them now. But here is a handful of somewhat less glamorous basics. Two of them take refrigerator staples and make them into versatile sauces. The others keep well. Some of my recipes call for them, and you'll find you will use them on your own, too.

■

PANTRY BASICS

Here are two *very* fast and flavorful recipes that perfectly complement meat and fish. The sauces are based on two American favorites: mustard and ketchup.

MUSTARD WINE SAUCE

In a small nonreactive saucepan, bring ½ cup dry white wine to a boil. Boil for 3 minutes.

Add 1 tablespoon Dijon mustard, 2 tablespoons minced parsley or chives and salt and freshly ground pepper to taste. Mix well. Bring to a boil and serve.

Clockwise from upper left: Gaufrette Potatoes, Carrot Basket, Leek Basket, zucchini basket, fried beet basket and Beet Chips, Crisp of Risotto, fried rice noodles, Asparagus Peelings, fried eggplant skin, Lotus Root Chips, fried basil leaves, Mushroom Chips, eggplant skin basket and fried horseradish.

KETCHUP SAUCE

In a small saucepan, melt 2 tablespoons sweet butter over medium heat and cook until golden brown.

Add 1 tablespoon ketchup, 3 tablespoons sherry vinegar and 1 tablespoon each of diced apple, capers, diced tomato and minced parsley. Add salt and freshly ground pepper to taste and mix well. Bring to a boil and serve.

NOTE: As good as this is with steak, chicken and pork chops, it is superb with sautéed or steamed skate, black bass, halibut and other strongly flavored fish.

■

BOUQUET GARNI

This is a small bundle of herbs that, immersed in a liquid, flavors it while it cooks. Remember to remove the Bouquet Garni before serving. You can add any herbs you like.

4-inch square of triple-thickness cheesecloth
¼ cup chopped leek (green part only)
1 bay leaf
Several sprigs thyme
Several sprigs parsley

Combine the herbs on the cheesecloth. Tie them up in the cheesecloth with kitchen string to make a secure bundle.

CLARIFIED BUTTER

Clarifying butter is a process that removes the milk solids, leaving a clear, deep yellow butter that is less apt to burn at higher temperatures.

1 cup sweet butter

Melt the butter in the top of a double boiler set over—not touching—boiling water. When the butter has melted completely, remove the top pan and let stand for 10 minutes. Skim as much of the white foam from the surface as possible. Let stand at room temperature 30 minutes longer.

Carefully pour the clear yellow butter into a clean container, leaving the milky solids behind. Or, strain the liquid through several layers of cheesecloth, rinsed in cool water and thoroughly wrung out, into a clean container. Store in the refrigerator, tightly covered, up to 2 months.

MAKES ¾ CUP

SIMPLE SYRUP

Ordinary granulated sugar sometimes doesn't dissolve completely. Use Simple Syrup as a substitute for granulated sugar. It ensures smooth (not grainy) results without sugar crystals.

2 cups water
2 cups sugar

Combine ingredients in a saucepan over medium heat. Bring to a boil, remove from heat and let cool. Pour into a clean glass jar. Store, tightly covered, in a kitchen cupboard. There is no need to refrigerate.

MAKES 3 CUPS

UNCOMMON GARNISHES

I always appreciated the little finishing touches that make a plate look truly dressed. But I prefer garnishes that add something more than visual amusement. Many of the flavored oils, of course, can be great fun—they are beautiful in themselves— and they taste wonderful. Here are two more ways to garnish: Fried Vegetable Accents, and a lovely old Provençal recipe for Sautéed Panisses.

FRIED VEGETABLE ACCENTS

When deep-fat fried, thinly sliced vegetables become crisp and yet keep both their color and flavor. You can prepare them hours in advance if you like, and they go a long way; just a few to a plate should be enough.

CELERY LEAVES

CELERIAC CHIPS

BEET CHIPS

CELERY JULIENNE

CARROT JULIENNE

ASPARAGUS PEELINGS

LOTUS ROOT CHIPS

MUSHROOM CHIPS

LEEK JULIENNE

EGGPLANT JULIENNE

LEEK / BEET / ZUCCHINI / LOTUS ROOT / EGGPLANT / OR
   CARROT BASKETS

Pat any moist vegetables dry with paper toweling.

Fry chips and juliennes at 350 to 375 degrees in 2 inches of vegetable oil, baskets in oil to cover.

Remove from the oil with a slotted spoon. The vegetables will be somewhat fragile and will become more crisp after being removed from the oil. Let cool slightly, then test for crispness. If not crisp enough, return them to the pot for a few seconds longer.

After frying, drain the vegetables on paper toweling and lightly salt.

CELERY LEAVES	Remove leaves from celery. Fry until crisp, about 10 seconds.
CELERIAC CHIPS	Peel the celeriac root and slice paper thin. Fry until crisp, about 30 seconds. Season with celery salt.
BEET CHIPS	Peel the beet and slice paper thin. Set on paper toweling and let dry for ½ hour. Lightly dust with flour, and shake off any excess. Fry until crisp, 15 to 20 seconds.
CELERY JULIENNE	Use very fine julienne. Lightly dust with flour and shake off any excess. Fry until crisp, about 10 seconds. Season with celery salt.
CARROT JULIENNE	Use very fine julienne. Lightly dust with flour and shake off any excess. Fry until crisp, about 10 seconds.

ASPARAGUS PEELINGS — With a vegetable peeler, thinly peel until all of the spear is used. Fry until crisp, about 10 seconds.

LOTUS ROOT CHIPS — Peel the lotus root and slice paper thin. Fry until crisp, about 15 seconds.

MUSHROOM CHIPS — Trim and thinly slice mushrooms. Fry until crisp, about 15 seconds.

LEEK JULIENNE — Use very fine julienne. Lightly dust with flour and shake off any excess. Fry until crisp, about 10 seconds.

EGGPLANT JULIENNE — Use very fine julienne. Lightly dust with flour and shake off any excess. Fry until crisp, about 10 seconds.

LEEK / BEET / ZUCCHINI / LOTUS ROOT / EGGPLANT OR CARROT BASKETS — Use very fine julienne. Lightly dust with flour and shake off any excess. Place in a small, round frying basket so as to cover the inside of the basket. Place a second basket over the vegetables, holding them in place. Fry until crisp, about 1 minute. Gently remove from the frying basket.

SAUTEED PANISSES

This Provençal specialty is something between a garnish and a side dish. Every piece is crunchy on the outside, creamy inside. Be sure not to make it more than ½ inch thick. Use canapé or cookie cutters to cut it out, or cut into shapes freehand.

1 quart milk
2 tablespoons sweet butter
Scant 2 cups chickpea flour
Salt and freshly ground pepper to taste
½ cup extra virgin olive oil

In a medium saucepan, bring the milk and butter to boil over medium-high heat. Slowly add the chickpea flour, whisking constantly. Simmer, stirring constantly, for 5 minutes. Mixture should be thick and free of lumps. Season with salt and pepper. Pour into a well-buttered 9-inch square pan. Refrigerate until set, about 10 minutes.

Cut into desired shapes. In a large sauté pan, heat the olive oil until hot. Add the pieces and cook until golden brown on all sides, about 2 minutes.

SERVES 4

CROSS-REFERENCE OF JUICES, VINAIGRETTES, OILS AND BROTHS

JUICES

ASPARAGUS	Lobster with Asparagus Juice
BEET	Beet-Ginger Oil
	Black Bass with Beet Juice and Caviar
BELL PEPPER	Bell Pepper Oil
BROCCOLI	Crab Cakes with Broccoli Juice
CARROT	Carrot-Cinnamon Oil
	Shrimp in Spicy Carrot Juice
	Spicy Carrot Juice
CELERY	Veal with Celery Juice and Roquefort Cheese
	Yellow Pike with Celery Juice
CHIVE	Chive Oil
DILL	Dill Oil
FENNEL	Smoked Salmon Custard with Fennel Juice
LEEK	Sea Scallops in Leek Juice
PINEAPPLE	Chicken in Pineapple Juice
TOMATO	Tomato Oil
RADISH	Cod with Pink Radish Juice
WATERCRESS	Watercress Oil

Shrimp Salad with Curry Oil (page 63)

ZUCCHINI	Lamb Canneloni with Zucchini Juice
	Sea Scallops with Zucchini Juice
	Zucchini Juice with Thyme

VINAIGRETTES

BASIL	Beef on a String with Basil Vinaigrette
	Salad of Crayfish, Zucchini and Tomato
CAVIAR	Buckwheat Pasta with Black Bass and Caviar
CITRUS	Salmon in Rice Paper with Citrus Vinaigrette
GINGER	Cold Sea Urchin Soufflé
	Lobster Couscous
	Sweetbread Fritters with Ginger Vinaigrette
HAZELNUT	Broccoli Mousse with Truffle Vinaigrette
	Chanterelle and Spinach Salad
	Sweetbreads with Yellow Potato Salad

JUNIPER	Wild Mushroom Gâteau
	Salmon Cabbage with Juniper Vinaigrette
LOBSTER	Open Ravioli with Shrimp
	Skate Wings with Artichokes
PEANUT	Broccoli Mousse with Truffle Vinaigrette
	Foie Gras with Fried Leeks
	Squab and Lentil Salad
SHRIMP	Open Ravioli with Shrimp
	Skate Wings with Artichokes
SOY AND GINGER	Asparagus Salad
	Duck Bricks
	Steamed Shrimp with Champagne Vinaigrette
	Veal in Rice Paper
TRUFFLE	Broccoli Mousse with Truffle Vinaigrette
	Duck Bricks

FLAVORED OILS

BELL PEPPER	Halibut with Truffle and Yellow Bell Pepper Oil
	"Spiked" Sweetbreads with Red Bell Pepper Oil
	Tuna Tartare with Assorted Oils and Chips
BEET-GINGER	Sautéed Calves' Liver with Beet-Ginger Oil
CARROT-CINNAMON	Soft Shell Crabs with Carrot-Cinnamon Oil
CHIVE	Millefeuille of Roquefort and Boursin
	Tuna Tartare with Assorted Oils and Chips

	Tuna Tartare with Gaufrette Potatoes
CINNAMON	Tempura with Cabbage Salad and Cinnamon Oil
CRANBERRY-ORANGE	Venison with Cranberry-Orange Oil
CURRY	Shrimp Salad with Curry Oil
	Tuna Tartare with Assorted Oils and Chips
DILL	Cold Cucumber Soup with Dill Oil
FENNEL	Marinated Lemon Chicken with Fennel Oil
GINGER	Beet-Ginger Oil
HORSERADISH	Cod in a Horseradish Crust
	Shrimp Skewers with Oysters and Horseradish Oil
LOBSTER	Grilled Veal with Lobster Béarnaise
	Lobster with Parsnip Purée
	Lobster Strudel
	Shrimp, Tomato and Cilantro Tart
	Terrine of Pasta and Crabmeat
MUSTARD	Rabbit Sausage with Mustard Oil
PEANUT	Whiting with Endive Broth
ROSEMARY	Goat Cheese Bricks with Endive Salad
	Salmon Leaves with Rosemary Oil
SAFFRON	Sea Scallops with Garlic and Saffron Oil
SHRIMP	Grilled Veal with Lobster Béarnaise
	Lobster with Parsnip Purée
	Lobster Strudel

	Shrimp, Tomato and Cilantro Tart
	Terrine of Pasta and Crabmeat
TOMATO	Red Snapper in Potato Flakes with Tomato Oil
	Sea Scallops with Garlic and Saffron Oil
TRUFFLE	Halibut with Truffle and Yellow Bell Pepper Oil
WATERCRESS	Goat Cheese with Watercress Oil

BROTHS

ARTICHOKE	Lamb with Artichokes and Olives
	Scallops with Artichoke Broth
ENDIVE	Whiting with Endive Broth
MIXED VEGETABLE	Black Bass in Zucchini Blossoms
	Buckwheat Pasta with Black Bass and Caviar
	Canneloni of Crab with Cardamom
	Cold Sea Urchin Soufflé

	Crisps of Risotto
	Lobster à la Nage
	Thai Chicken Soup with Coconut Milk
MUSHROOM BROTH	Foie Gras with Fried Leeks
	Marble of Foie Gras
	Soufflé of Foie Gras
MUSHROOM SYRUP	Breast of Pheasant Parmentier
	Lamb in a Potato Crust
	Lamb with Wild Mushrooms
	Lobster with Parsnip Purée
	Monkfish with Mushroom Syrup
	Salmon in a Shiitake Shell
	Sautéed Foie Gras and Potato Terrine
	Squab and Lentil Salad
	Squab Purse
	Truffled Lamb with Fava Bean Purée
SHALLOT	Shallot Broth with Flounder
VEGETABLE	Beef on a String with Basil Vinaigrette
WATERCRESS	Watercress Broth with Yellow Rice

INDEX

■

ABOUT THE AUTHOR

At the age of sixteen, Jean-Georges began training in his native Alsace, in the kitchens of L'Auberge de l'Ill. The great restaurant of Paul and Jean-Pierre Haeberlin is virtually a shrine for Alsatians and all of France. Four years at Paul's side taught Jean-Georges the fundamentals of classic French cuisine, and from even the earliest days of his apprenticeship, Jean-Georges realized how fortunate he was to learn from true masters of French cuisine.

His good fortune continued in the years that followed. Jean-Georges worked with extraordinary talents: the legendary Paul Bocuse, the innovative Eckart Witzigmann in Munich and finally Louis Outhier of L'Oasis in La Napoule-Plage on the French Riviera. Outhier sent Jean-Georges to Europe, America and the Far East as the leader of his "flying squadron of chefs," to learn from a world of ingredients and techniques. Much of what delighted him abroad has become part of his cuisine today, and Jean-Georges says of Louis Outhier, "it was he who encouraged me to trust my instincts."

In 1984, Outhier installed Jean-Georges as chef of his newly created "Marquis" in Boston, which was quickly recognized as one of the leading restaurants. Then, in 1985, Louis Outhier asked Jean-Georges to join him as chef in his most ambitious project: Restaurant Lafayette in New York City.

Jean-Georges quickly learned that the tastes and desires of an American clientele were not the same as in France; New Yorkers seemed to be in more of a hurry, unaccustomed to lingering two and a half or three hours over lunch, and at times it seemed they rushed through dinner. Beyond this, he noticed they were mindful of their health and concerned about the calories of classic French cuisine.

One morning in 1987, while making himself a glass of carrot juice, Jean-Georges was inspired to try the fresh vegetable juice as a sauce for shellfish. He warmed the carrot juice, seasoned it with a pat of sweet butter and cayenne pepper, and served it as a substitute for a traditional sauce with large, lightly steamed shrimp. It was absolutely delicious. From then on he was determined to approach cooking from an entirely different direction.

Over the next three years, Jean-Georges' cooking moved further away from classic French cuisine. Today, having earned the *New York Times'* highest rating of four stars, Jean-Georges offers a menu at Lafayette that faithfully reflects his new approach, with the various dishes separated under four simple "basics" of the cooking he brings you today: Juices, Flavored Oils, Vinaigrettes and Broths.

At thirty-three, Jean-Georges is already an acclaimed four-star chef and considered to be among the leading, most innovative chefs in the United States. He creates new recipes endlessly. It was with regret that we were obliged to turn some away, marvelous as they were, so that this book could at last go to print. Those who have enjoyed the pleasure of eating at Jean-Georges' table know that his thoughts on food never stand still for long. Happily, today we can take some of his ideas and simple techniques home with us and enjoy them on our own with family and friends.

CREDITS

Pages 72, 92 and 106: La Cornue stove courtesy of Europe and USA, P.O. Box 330532, Miami, Fl. 33233–0532

Pages 82 and 83: table and chair courtesy of Zona, New York

Page 120: table courtesy of Cobweb, New York

Page 132: Japanese tea cups courtesy of Jomon Gallery, New York

Pages 138 and 139: sushi tray courtesy of Jomon Gallery, New York; lacquer box and lacquer service bowl courtesy of Teruyo Mory, New York

Pages 174 and 175: glasses courtesy of Pottery Barn, New York

Page 180: table and pewter platter courtesy of Cobweb, New York